Audrey Grant's
BETTER BRIDGE

♠ ♥ ♦ ♠ ♠ ♥ ♦ ♣ ♠ ♥ ♦ ♣ ♠ ♥ ♦ ♠ ♠ ♥ ♦ ♣ ♠ ♥ ♦ ♣ ♠ ♥ ♦ ♣

Bidding

CENTENNIAL PRESS

ISBN 0–8220–1666–4

Copyright © 1995 by Audrey Grant

Printed in U.S.A.
All Rights Reserved

Design and composition by
John Reinhardt Book Design

Centennial Press
Box 82087, Lincoln, Nebraska 68501
an imprint of Cliffs Notes, Inc.

♠ ♥ ♦ ♣

To all the bridge teachers.
Your dedication, skill, and professionalism
have made me proud to be counted among you.

Contents

Contents

Part 4
THE PLOT THICKENS—ALL ABOUT REBIDS

Part 5

WHEN BOTH SIDES HAVE SOMETHING TO SAY

Part 7

CONVENTIONS

Preface

For many years, I've seen people of all ages and all walks of life playing bridge. These bridge players are so obviously enjoying themselves that I've made it part of my life's work to teach and write about the game.

The best theorists in the world have shared their secrets with me, and I bring these pieces of bridge wisdom to you in a manner which I hope you will find readable.

Bridge is more than a game. It's a wonderful life skill. It's given me—as it can you—friends around the world. Anywhere you travel, being able to play a hand of bridge opens the door to meeting new people.

Here's more good news about bridge. It's healthy. The days of smoke-filled rooms of bridge players are long gone. It's accepted now that bridge exercises the mind the same way that physical activity exercises your body. That's right. Research indicates that the brain actually changes in response to the stimulus which a game like bridge provides.

This second book in the series covers standard bidding practices common in North America and most other parts of the world. You'll find yourself grasping the principles behind sound bidding practice, and you'll feel much more comfortable with a variety of partners.

There's material in this book which will help you to improve your bidding judgment. It gives you a firm basis from which to evolve. Bidding is about getting to the best contract, and this book gives you the tools to do just that in the most straightforward manner.

I like to keep my bidding conversations simple, yet accurate. I want both my partner and myself to be comfortable during the auction. I want to experience the excitement of the conversation, without the stress. As I've often said, I don't want a point or two to come between friends. I hope you'll feel the same way after reading this book.

Audrey Grant

Acknowledgments

To my husband, David Lindop, who works hand-in-hand with me in all my bridge endeavors. Without his talent, drive, and love, these books would still be in the conceptual stage.

To my mother, Connie, who became an expert in counting up to thirteen while making sure every card was in its place.

To my dad, Alex, who writes my bridge jokes—and that's no laughing matter.

To my children, Joanna and Jason, who get involved in so many aspects of the projects—from making crepes for the bridge students to dressing up as cards.

To my brother, Brian, who has helped test much of the material used throughout this series.

To Julie Greenberg, head of the Education Department at the American Contract Bridge League, for her friendship and inspiration, and to the members of her staff for sharing their knowledge about bridge instruction.

To Henry Francis, editor of the *American Contract Bridge League Bulletin,* and his staff, who have been editing my work for years and have helped turn me into a better writer.

To Jerry Helms, the true bridge professional, who has generously shared both his teaching methods and expertise.

To Pat Harrington, whose understanding of the beginners' point of view has helped me write with more clarity to the books.

To Eric Rodwell and Zia Mahmood, world-class players, who have spent countless hours sharing their theories about the game.

To Fred Gitelman and Sheri Winestock, for showing what bridge will look like in the 21st Century.

To Michael Laughlin and Kirk Frederick, for their belief in me, together with their creative input.

To Flip Wilson, for his confidence that even my wildest promotional ideas would work out.

To the American Contract Bridge League Board of Directors, who help provide an overview of how bridge is played in all parts of the country.

To Doug Lincoln, for his vision and his ongoing support of this project.

To Jim Borthwick, who took care of all the details to bring this series to fruition.

To Michele Spence, for the many hours spent proof-reading each page of the manuscript and her cheerful disposition throughout the project.

To John Reinhardt, for combining his bridge knowledge and design talents to make each book in the series pleasing to the eye.

And of course, I'd like to acknowledge all those students, teachers, and expert players who have constantly provided inspiration and ideas in the field of bridge.

Part 1

INTRODUCTION TO BIDDING

Valuing Your Hand

"Don't let a point or two come between friends."

I was brought up on a farm, and after dinner we would spend many a memorable summer evening playing baseball. If you played with us, a home run was from the bush to the tree and back. When we left the farm, we didn't expect our version of baseball to be widespread. Those were our house rules.

There are house rules for bridge. They don't need to be discussed in detail because they vary from one part of the country to the next. They may or may not be based on sound bridge theory.

Bridge is bidding, play and defense. The most controversial part of the game is the bidding. Keep an open mind when discussing bidding theories. Above all, don't let a point or two come between friends.

In any card game, you like to know if you have a good hand. Bridge is a game of taking tricks, so you want to know the trick-taking potential of your hand. Tricks are generally won with *high cards*—aces, kings, queens, and jacks—and sometimes with the lower-ranking cards from long suits. The first step in valuing a bridge hand, therefore, is to look at the high cards and the length of the suits.

High Card Points

The high cards are given an estimated value referred to as *high card points (HCPs)*. There's not much controversy over this part of the evaluation and, whether you're playing on an ice floe in the Arctic or on a sailboat in Florida, there's general agreement on the relative point count assigned to the high cards. You're probably familiar with this scale:

High Card Points

Ace	4 points
King	3 points
Queen	2 points
Jack	1 point

High card points are a guide, and could change. Some computer programs, for example, assign 4.3 to an ace, trying for more accuracy in hand valuation. Who knows, in the future the queen may be worth 3 points, and the king might be demoted to 2 points—but don't hold your breath on this particular possibility.

Distribution Points

The second part of valuing a hand is to take the *distribution* into account. Distribution can be looked at from two points of view. You can focus on the long suits or the short suits. Some players, when making the opening bid, give a *void* 3 points, a *singleton* 2 points and a *doubleton* 1 point. This isn't my preference. Experience and expert advice suggest that it's more reliable to value the long suits when opening the bidding. Short suits have merit, but only after a suitable trump suit has been found. Evaluate the distribution in this manner:

Distribution Points

Five-card suit	Add 1 point
Six-card suit	Add 2 points
Seven-card suit	Add 3 points

Call me if you get an eight-card suit, even long distance if it's a nine-card suit—and reverse the charges if you get a ten-card suit or longer.

The Total Value

The total value of the hand is the combination of high card points and distribution points.

	High Card Points	*Distribution Points*	*Total Points*
♠ A K 8	7	0	7
♥ Q J 7	3	0	3
♦ 10 8	0	0	0
♣ 9 6 5 3 2	0	1	1
	10 +	1 =	11

If you value shortness rather than length, you would get 1 point for the doubleton diamond instead of 1 point for the five-card club suit—you don't count points for both length and shortness. The net result would still be 11 total points. Here's another example of valuing a hand:

	High Card Points	*Distribution Points*	*Total Points*
♠ 7	0	0	0
♥ K Q J 7 3	6	1	7
♦ K 10 3 2	3	0	3
♣ A J 5	5	0	5
	14 +	1 =	15

Instead of 1 point for the five-card heart suit, you could count 2 points for the singleton spade. That would give you an estimate of 16 points for the strength of the hand, rather than 15 points. A difference of one or two points isn't going to matter much in the long run. There are other factors which can affect the value of a hand, and these are sometimes more important than HCPs and distribution. When opening the bidding, length rather than shortness is used consistently throughout the book for valuing distribution. When supporting partner's suit, rather than opening the bidding, valuing shortness can become important. This is discussed in later chapters.

Some players count length when bidding notrump; others don't. My recommendation is to value the hand using length points when opening the bidding regardless of whether you plan to start the bidding in notrump or a suit.

Whichever valuation style you prefer, the result will be about the same.

Five Hints to Improve Your Judgment

There's more to valuing a hand than adding up the high card points and the distribution points. You might have heard it said that you need to use your judgment. Here are five factors to take into account when valuing a hand.

1. Togetherness

Hands were once valued using *quick tricks.* An ace represented a quick trick because it was fairly certain to take a trick. An ace-king combination in a suit was worth two quick tricks. A king by itself, without the ace or queen, may or may not end up taking a trick, so it was considered to be worth half a quick trick.

The concept of quick tricks isn't used much anymore. Consideration of the trick-taking potential of a hand, however, should take into account the togetherness of the high cards. Compare these two hands:

```
1) ♠ K 9 8 5 3        2) ♠ A K Q 9 8
   ♥ A Q                 ♥ 5 3
   ♦ Q 10 6              ♦ K Q 10
   ♣ K 7 2              ♣ 7 6 2
```

Both hands have 14 high card points and 1 distribution point. The point count valuation of the hands would suggest that they're equal. A closer look, focusing on where the high cards are located, brings to light a different story. On the first hand, there's only one sure trick, the ♥A. The other high cards may take tricks, but it will depend on where the missing high cards are located. On the second hand there are three or more spade tricks, and at least one diamond trick. There's much more trick-taking potential when the high cards are working together than when they're isolated in different suits.

2. The Supporting Cast

High cards are the stars within each suit. The lower cards also have their role to play. Compare these two hands:

1) ♠ K 7 2	2) ♠ K 10 8
♥ A J 6	♥ A J 10
♦ K Q 4	♦ K Q 10
♣ Q J 5 2	♣ Q J 10 9

Both hands have 16 points, and the high cards are located in the same suits. Only the low cards differ, but the second hand feels much stronger than the first hand. Look at the club suit, for example. In the first hand, you may or may not be able to develop club tricks depending on the location of the missing high cards. In the second hand, you expect to take two club tricks because the ♣10 and ♣9 go along with the queen-jack combination.

The intermediate cards can make a hand more valuable. You might not take them into account when initially valuing a hand. If it comes down to a close decision on whether or not to bid, this is one of the factors that might sway your judgment.

3. Location, Location, Location

The value of a hand is dynamic, and may change during the course of the *auction*. For example, suppose you have this hand:

♠ 5
♥ Q 8 7 2
♦ A K J 5 3
♣ K 5 3

As the opening bidder, you would value this hand as 14 points—

13 HCPs plus 1 for the five-card diamond suit—and open the bidding 1♦. Partner responds 1♥. Now the hand has improved in value. You have good support for partner's suit, the ♥Q is likely to be of value, and the singleton spade should also prove useful. Revaluing your hand to take all this into account will be discussed later.

Suppose, instead, partner responds 1♠. Now the singleton spade is more a liability than an asset. You haven't yet found a fit with partner, and will have to proceed cautiously in the auction.

If the opponent on your left were to bid 2♣, the value of the ♣K would drop considerably. It's now likely that the ♣A is held by your left-hand opponent, and your king will probably not take a trick. On the other hand, if the opponent on your right were to bid clubs, the ♣K would rise in value. With the ♣A probably located on your right, the king is more likely to take a trick.

4. The Shape of Things

The pattern, or shape, of the hand can be important. Some hands are *balanced*. They have no voids or singletons and at most one doubleton. Other hands are *unbalanced* and are generally more suitable for play in suit contracts. For example, here are three unbalanced hand patterns:

```
X X X X X      X X X X X X      X X X X X X X
X X X X X      X X X X         X X X X X
X X            X X             X
X              X              —

5-5-2-1        6-4-2-1         7-5-1-0
```

The more unbalanced a hand becomes, the more challenging it is to evaluate. Long suits can improve the trick-taking potential of a hand. Compare these two hands:

```
1) ♠ K Q J          2) ♠ K Q J 10 9
   ♥ A 10 9            ♥ A 4
   ♦ 10 9 4 3          ♦ 3
   ♣ A Q J            ♣ A Q J 10 9
```

The high cards in both hands are the same, but the trick-taking potential of the second hand is much greater than that of the first hand. With the first hand, you might expect two spade tricks, one heart trick, and a couple of club tricks—five tricks in total. With the second hand, you might take four spade tricks, a heart trick, and at least four club tricks—nine tricks. Of course, you'll take all these tricks only if your side plays the hand. You won't take nearly as many tricks if the opponents are playing in a heart or diamond contract. So the tricks from long suits are referred to as *playing tricks*.

The trick-taking potential from long suits is partly taken into consideration by giving distribution points for long suits. The value of long suits, however, increases dramatically as hands become very unbalanced. As an extreme example, suppose a hand contained all thirteen spades. That's only 10 HCPs plus 9 extra points for the 13-card suit, a total of 19 points. But you can take all the tricks with spades as the trump suit! So, judgment tells you that there's more to hand valuation than simply adding up the high card points and distribution points.

5. High Cards in Short Suits

Another subject that often comes up is the value of high cards when they're in short suits. What if one of the high cards is a singleton? Is it sound to value a singleton king, for example, as three points when, in fact, it may have no trick-taking value? What value is a doubleton queen? Consider how these two hands fit together:

PARTNER'S HAND
♠ 8 7 6 5 2
♥ Q 6
♦ A J 8 4
♣ Q 4

YOUR HAND
♠ Q 4
♥ K J 10 8 7 5 2
♦ K
♣ J 7 2

Your doubleton ♠Q is practically worthless. It won't help you take tricks in the spade suit or prevent the opponents from taking their tricks in the suit. On the other hand, partner's ♥Q, even though it's a doubleton, is very valuable since it fits nicely with your heart suit.

The ♦K is not a very useful card. A small singleton diamond would be just as valuable because the opponents would still not be able to take any tricks in the suit if hearts is the trump suit. On this hand, the ♠K or ♣K would be of more value than the ♦K.

By themselves, neither the ♣Q nor the ♣J are very useful cards. The way they work together on this hand, however, prevents the opponents from taking the first three tricks in the suit—if the opponents take the first two tricks with the ♣A and ♣K, your ♣J will be the highest remaining club.

Rather than getting too complicated, I prefer to count the high cards for what they're worth, whether or not they're in short suits. That works well if you value length rather than shortness for distribution. Either the high cards or the shortness will be valuable, but not both.

Summary

To bid well, you need a feeling for the trick-taking potential of a hand. As a guideline, use the following scale to estimate the value of your hand:

High Card Points		Distribution Points	
Ace	4 points	5-card suit	1 point
King	3 points	6-card suit	2 points
Queen	2 points	7-card suit	3 points
Jack	1 point		

Add the high card points to the distribution points to determine the value of the hand. Be flexible. Remember that this is only a starting guideline. There are other factors that can play a part in the value of a hand, and the value can go up or down during the auction. Develop judgment by taking the following five factors into consideration:

1. The increased value of high cards that work together.
2. The importance of intermediate cards.
3. The changing value of high cards as the auction progresses.
4. The influence of long suits and unbalanced distribution.
5. The possible diminished value of high cards in short suits.

Exercises

1. What is the point count value for each of the following hands?

a) ♠ K 9 6
   ♥ Q J 8 4
   ♦ A 10 6
   ♣ K Q J

b) ♠ 8 2
   ♥ K Q 9 7 3
   ♦ A K J
   ♣ 10 8 3

c) ♠ J 10 8
   ♥ 6
   ♦ A Q 10 8 6 5 3
   ♣ K 5

d) ♠ Q J 8 7 6
   ♥ 9 8 6 4 2
   ♦ K Q
   ♣ 6

e) ♠ K 10
   ♥ Q J 9 8 6 4
   ♦ A J 5
   ♣ 9 3

f) ♠ K Q J
   ♥ A J
   ♦ A Q 9
   ♣ K J 10 7 4

2. The value of each of the following hands is 14 points. Compare each pair of hands. In each case, which hand do you feel has more trick-taking potential, i) or ii)?

a)   i) ♠ 7 3
       ♥ K Q J 10 2
       ♦ 8 5
       ♣ A K 8 2

    ii) ♠ K 3
       ♥ Q 8 7 5 2
       ♦ A J
       ♣ K 10 8 2

b)   i) ♠ K
       ♥ A 9 8 6 3
       ♦ Q J
       ♣ Q 9 6 4 3

    ii) ♠ 3
       ♥ A Q J 6 3
       ♦ 8 3
       ♣ K Q 9 6 4

c)   i) ♠ K J 5 4 3
       ♥ 2
       ♦ A J 7 5 4
       ♣ K 2

    ii) ♠ K J 10 9 8
       ♥ 2
       ♦ A J 10 9 7
       ♣ K 9

d)   i) ♠ 4
       ♥ K Q 10 8 7 6
       ♦ A Q 10 6 4
       ♣ 6

    ii) ♠ A 4 3
       ♥ K Q 10 8
       ♦ Q 10 6 4
       ♣ K 6

3. You're sitting South with this hand:

a) ♠ Q J 8 7
   ♥ –
   ♦ K 9 6
   ♣ A J 10 8 5 3

a) What would be the value of this hand if you were the opening bidder?

Has the value of the hand increased or decreased as a result of the following auctions:

b)	WEST	NORTH	EAST	SOUTH (YOU)
				1♣
	Pass	1♥	Pass	?

c)	WEST	NORTH	EAST	SOUTH (YOU)
				1♣
	Pass	1♠	Pass	?

d)	WEST	NORTH	EAST	SOUTH (YOU)
				1♣
	1♦	Pass	1♠	?

e)	WEST	NORTH	EAST	SOUTH (YOU)
				1♣
	1♥	1♠	2♦	?

Answers to Exercises

1a) **16 points**. There are only HCPs, no distribution points.

1b) **14 points**. There are 13 HCPs plus 1 for the five-card heart suit.

1c) **13 points**. There are 10 HCPs plus 3 for the seven-card diamond suit.

1d) **10 points**. There are 8 HCPs plus 1 for each of the five-card suits.

1e) **13 points**. There are 11 HCPs plus 2 points for the six-card suit.

1f) **22 points**. There are 21 HCPs plus 1 point for the five-card suit.

2a) **i.** In the first hand, the high cards are together. In the second hand, the high cards are isolated.

2b) **ii.** The second hand has no high cards in short suits.

2c) **ii.** The second hand has more intermediate cards (tens and nines) than the first.

2d) **i.** In the first hand, the long suits provide a lot of trick-taking potential, even though there is one less king than in the second hand.

3a) **13 points**. There are 11 HCPs plus 2 points for the six-card club suit.

3b) The value of the hand has **decreased**. The heart void is likely to be a liability if that's where partner's strength lies.

3c) The value of the hand has **increased**. There's support for partner's suit, the ♠Q and ♠J are likely to be useful cards, and the heart void will likely be useful if spades is the trump suit.

3d) The hand has **decreased** in value. The ♦K is less likely to take a trick, and the spade suit is unlikely to provide much trick-taking potential.

3e) The hand has **increased** in value. There's good support for partner's suit, the heart shortness should be useful, since that's the opponents' suit, and it sounds as though the ♦K is favorably placed.

The Bidding Process

"Bridge is a combination of skill, luck, and your relationship with your partner."

Bridge is a partnership game, and nowhere is this of more importance than during the auction. Both partners have a role to play. They keep the overall objective in sight—reaching a reasonable contract. To do this successfully, they become familiar with the language of bidding, so that they can send information to partner, and in turn, receive and interpret partner's messages.

The Target

Through the bidding process, the partnership has to come up with the answers to two questions:

- Where's the best place for the partnership to play the contract—a trump suit or notrump?
- What's the best level—partscore, game, or slam?

These questions are interconnected. You can't decide whether to play in a suit contract or notrump without knowing the level; and

---

you can't know the level without knowing whether you're playing in a suit or notrump. Let's start by answering the questions one at a time, and then see how we can put them together.

Finding Your Fit

To suggest playing in a trump suit, the partnership wants to have more combined cards in the suit than the opponents. You need at least seven cards to have a majority. Even if you do have seven combined cards in a suit, the opponents have six, nearly as many as you. It's much more comfortable to have eight or more combined cards to consider playing with that suit as trump.

The Eight-Card Fit

When you and your partner hold eight or more combined cards in a suit, this can be considered a suitable trump suit. It's referred to as an *eight-card fit.*

The eight cards could be divided in different ways. There could be four in each hand. One player could have five, and the other three. In the most extreme case, there could be eight cards in one hand, and none in the other. Imagine the auction if you held all eight cards, and your partner had none. It would be a challenge to keep your eyebrows from getting closer and closer to your hairline as you bid and rebid the suit. Fortunately, that doesn't happen too often.

An eight-card fit usually refers to eight or more combined cards in a suit. Anything beyond eight is a bonus. Much of the bidding process will be centered around uncovering suitable trump fits.

Less Than Perfect

There are times when you might have to settle for a less than perfect fit. The bidding process will not always provide enough room to explore all the possibilities, and a strong six-card or seven-card fit might prove adequate when the length is concentrated in one hand. Consider this layout of the heart suit:

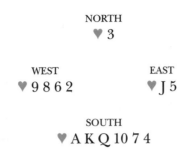

NORTH
♥ 3

WEST   EAST
♥ 9 8 6 2   ♥ J 5

SOUTH
♥ A K Q 10 7 4

North-South have only a seven-card fit, but South's hearts are long enough and strong enough to serve as a trump suit. This is the exception, rather than the rule. Generally, you want to find a trump suit that's fairly evenly divided between the partnership hands, providing flexibility for such things as traveling back and forth between the two hands.

Length, Not Strength

Notice that nothing was said about the strength of the fit, only the length. In choosing a trump suit, length is more important than strength. Compare the spade and heart suits in the following hand:

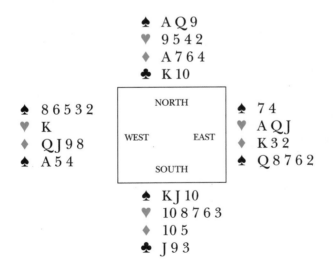

♠ A Q 9
♥ 9 5 4 2
♦ A 7 6 4
♣ K 10

♠ 8 6 5 3 2   NORTH   ♠ 7 4
♥ K   ♥ A Q J
♦ Q J 9 8   WEST   EAST   ♦ K 3 2
♣ A 5 4   ♣ Q 8 7 6 2
                     SOUTH

♠ K J 10
♥ 10 8 7 6 3
♦ 10 5
♣ J 9 3

North-South have the top six cards in the spade suit. East-West have only small cards. Spades, however, would make a poor trump suit for North-South. After three rounds of the suit have been played, West would have two remaining trump.

On the other hand, East-West have the top four cards in the heart suit. Nonetheless, hearts would be an excellent trump suit for North-South. After three rounds of the suit are played, all the East-West trump will have gone. North will still have one trump left, and South will have two left.

It's not the location of the high cards that's important. Whatever the trump suit, North-South will still have three tricks with the high cards in the spade suit, and will have to lose three tricks in the heart suit. It will be the low cards that will make a difference in a trump contract.

Finding Your Level

The way the scoring works affects the bidding. Not all contracts at the same level are worth the same amount. For the *minors suits*—clubs and diamonds—you get 20 points per trick. For the *major suits*—hearts and spades—you get 30 points per trick. Notrump contracts are worth 40 points for the first trick, and 30 points for each trick thereafter.

Bidding and making a contract of 3♣ is worth a trick score of 60 points (20 + 20 + 20). A contract of 3♥ has a trick score of 90 points (30 + 30 + 30), and a contract of 3NT is worth 100 points (40 + 30 + 30). This difference in scoring has a big impact on the target you try to reach.

The Bonus Levels

A contract with a trick score worth less than 100 points is referred to as a *partscore* contract. A contract worth 100 or more points is referred to as a *game* contract. For bidding and making a game contract you receive a bonus. The details of the scoring are left to the appendix, but the important point is that these contracts take on a special significance:

3NT   4♥   4♠   5♣   5♦

They're the lowest contracts in each of the suits or notrump that are worth 100 or more points. Anything less is a partscore contract. A contract of 4♣, for example, is worth only 80 points, and is a partscore contract even though you need to take one more trick than in the game contract of 3NT. A contract of 5♥ would also be a game contract, but it would be unnecessary—and perhaps risky—to bid to this level to receive the game bonus.

The other bonus levels don't depend on the trick score. A *small slam* is any contract at the six level—6♣ or 6♥, for example. You need to take twelve of the thirteen tricks. A *grand slam* is any contract at the seven level, where you need to take all thirteen tricks—7♦ or 7NT, for example. The partnership receives a considerable bonus for bidding and making a slam contract.

Slam contracts are infrequent, and the usual decision the partnership has to make is between staying in a partscore contract or going for the game bonus level. Let's look at the main guideline the partnership uses when making this decision.

Important Numbers

For the partnership to decide on an appropriate level for the contract, it needs to know about the combined strength of the hands. This is simply a matter of adding together the value of each hand. A large part of the bidding process will involve exchanging enough information, so that at least one of the partners has a good estimate of the combined assets of the partnership.

Experience has shown that the approximate relationship between points and the target level is the following:

- 26 combined points are required for game in a major suit (ten tricks) or notrump (nine tricks).
- 29 combined points are required for a minor suit game (eleven tricks).
- 33 combined points are required for a small slam (twelve tricks).
- 37 combined points are required for a grand slam (all thirteen tricks).

This relationship between points and tricks governs most of the decisions the partnership makes during the auction. In its most basic form:

- With 26 or more combined points, the partnership targets for the game level. With less, the partnership should stop in partscore.

Most of the rest of this book will focus on how the bidding process can be used to find out whether or not the partnership has 26 or more points.

Why 26?

The point count value of a hand is merely a way of estimating its strength. There are other factors that can be taken into account. Some game contracts can be made with fewer than 26 combined points. Since 3NT requires only nine tricks, it can often be made when there are as few as 24 or 25 combined points. On the other hand, 27 or 28 points might not be enough to make a game if the hands don't fit well together.

The requirement of 26 points for a game-level contract is merely a guideline. It's a signpost to point you in the right direction: with less than 26 points, aim for a partscore contract; with 26 or more points, aim for at least a game contract.

Ten to Nine

Why can you take ten tricks in a major suit with the same strength required to take nine tricks in notrump? The secret lies in the power of a trump suit. A small card in the trump suit can have the power of an ace. You can use the trump suit to stop the opponents from taking a lot of tricks in their longest and strongest suit. You can trump tricks that would otherwise be lost to the opponents' high cards.

Sometimes you can take two or three more tricks playing in a trump suit than you can playing the same hand in notrump. At other times, the same number of tricks are available. On balance, you should be able to take at least one more trick in an eight-card or longer fit than in notrump.

Putting It Together

When it comes time to decide on the contract, the partnership takes into consideration both the trump fit and the target level. Let's see how this works.

At the Partscore Level

Playing in an eight-card or longer fit will usually provide at least one or two more tricks than in a notrump contract, so, at the partscore level, the partnership can use the following guideline:

- Play partscore contracts in an eight-card or longer trump fit. Without a trump fit, play in notrump.

Notrump and major suit contracts often take preference over minor suit contracts, even at the partscore level, because they have a higher trick score.

At the Game Level

3NT contracts require nine tricks while 4♥ or 4♠ contracts require ten tricks. Playing in a suit contract, however, usually allows you to take at least one and maybe several more tricks than playing in a notrump contract. The general guideline is:

- At the game level, play in 4♥ or 4♠ with an eight-card or longer trump fit. Otherwise, play in 3NT.

Forget those minor suits! Because minor suits are worth only 20 points per trick, it takes eleven tricks to make game in a minor suit. That's why minor suit games require 29 or more points. Only nine tricks are required to make game in a notrump contract, and you can expect to make 3NT if you have as few as 26 combined points. For this reason, you should generally **play game in 3NT rather than 5♣ or 5♦ , even if you have a fit in a minor suit**.

Look at it this way: If you can take exactly ten tricks on a hand, would you rather be playing in a contract of 3NT making an overtrick or 5♣ or 5♦ going down one trick? I'd forget about those minor suit games.

At the Slam Level

Since all slam contracts require the same number of tricks, you want to find a trump fit whenever possible. The guideline at this level is:

- Play slam contracts in an eight-card or longer trump fit. Without a trump fit, play in notrump.

The Partnership Roles

To determine the denomination—trump suit or notrump—and the level—partscore, game, or slam—the partners exchange enough information about their strength and distribution, so that at least one member of the partnership is in a position to place the contract.

The opening bidder starts off describing the hand and continues to fill in the picture as the auction progresses. As such, opener plays the role of a narrator, telling the story of the hand. Opener's partner, the responder, tends to play more the role of a reporter, listening to what opener has to say, and urging opener to complete the description of the hand.

The bidding can proceed in many directions. Sometimes it will be responder who knows more about the combined hands; at other times it will be opener. Whichever partner ends up with this knowledge must now play the role of captain, guiding the partnership to a suitable contract.

At some point during the auction, one of the players will usually make a bid that limits the hand to a narrow range of strength and distribution. Partner now becomes the captain, and has the responsibility for placing the contract. Such *limit bids* are an important part of the bidding process, and make it easier for the partnership to agree on the level and denomination.

The Traffic Lights

The bidding conversation is much more comfortable when both partners understand the messages conveyed by each bid. In addition to saying something about strength and distribution, each bid falls into one of three categories:

> *Sign-off Bid*—A bid which asks partner to pass. This usually occurs when one partner has limited the strength and distribution of the hand and the other partner, as captain, is placing the contract.
>
> *Invitational Bid*—A bid which gives partner the choice of bidding again or passing. This usually occurs when one partner makes a limit bid, narrowly describing the strength and distribution, leaving the choice of final contract to the other partner.
>
> *Forcing Bid*—A bid which asks partner to bid again. This usually occurs when one partner has insufficient information to place the contract, and requires further information.

These messages are like the colors of a traffic signal, telling you whether to stop, proceed with caution, or go. As the bidding process is discussed in the upcoming chapters, you'll start to see the importance of the bidding messages. You'll feel much more in control if you recognize the message conveyed through partner's bid. Is it sign-off, invitational, or forcing?

Summary

During the bidding process, the partners work together to find out whether the contract should be played in a trump suit or in notrump, and the target level to which they should be aspiring—partscore, game, or slam. The opening bidder gets the first chance to start describing the strength and distribution of the hand. Opener's partner, the responder, listens to opener's story and provides further information while giving opener an opportunity to finish the description of the hand. Each bid the partnership makes sends one of three messages:

- Sign-off—Partner is expected to pass.
- Invitational—Partner has the choice of bidding again or passing.
- Forcing—Partner is expected to bid again.

As soon as one partner limits the strength and distribution of the hand to a narrow range, the other partner takes on the role of captain, and places the contract using the following guidelines:

- With less than 26 combined points, play a partscore contract in any eight-card or longer trump fit. With no fit, play partscore in notrump.
- With 26 or more combined points play a game contract in 4♥ or 4♠ with an eight-card or longer trump fit. With no major suit fit, play in 3NT.
- With 33 or more combined points, play a small slam contract in any eight-card or longer trump suit. With no fit, play slam in notrump.
- With 37 or more combined points, play a grand slam contract in any eight-card or longer trump suit. With no fit, play slam in notrump.

Exercises

1. Suppose your partner describes a hand that contains from 13 to 15 points. What should be the target level for the partnership—partscore, game, or slam—when you hold each of the following hands?

a)		b)		c)	
♠	K 7 3	♠	A Q J 4	♠	A 4
♥	Q 8 4	♥	9 2	♥	A Q 10 8
♦	10 7 5 3	♦	K Q 8 4	♦	K Q J
♣	Q J 7	♣	A 10 5	♣	K J 9 5

2. Suppose your partner describes a hand that contains three spades, five hearts, two diamonds, and three clubs. Does the partnership have a suitable trump suit to play in when you hold each of the following hands?

a)		b)		c)	
♠	A 10 5	♠	A 6 5 2	♠	K J 8 6 4
♥	9 6	♥	K 9 2	♥	Q 10 9 6
♦	K 10 8 6	♦	K J 9 7 5	♦	J 4
♣	J 9 5 4	♣	4	♣	K 8

3. Partner opens the bidding 1NT describing a hand with 16–18 points and at least two cards in each suit but at most five cards in any suit. As captain, where would you place the contract when you hold each of the following hands?

a)		b)		c)	
♠	Q J 9 7 6 2	♠	9	♠	K 7
♥	8 5	♥	K Q 10 7 6 3	♥	10 5
♦	9 7 3	♦	A 9 7	♦	A 10 8 7 3
♣	6 3	♣	J 4 3	♣	Q 10 9 4

Answers to Exercises

1a) **Partscore**. You have 8 HCPs, and partner has at most 15. The maximum number of combined points the partnership holds is 23.

1b) **Game**. You have 16 HCPs. The combined partnership strength is 29, 30, or 31 points. That's enough for a game level contract but not enough for a slam contract.

1c) **Small Slam**. You have 20 HCPs, so the partnership has at least 33 combined points and at most 35 combined points. This lies within the range for a small slam contract.

2a) **No**. There's no eight-card or longer suit between the combined hands.

2b) **Yes**. The partnership has an eight-card heart fit.

2c) **Yes**. The partnership has both an eight-card spade fit and a nine-card heart fit. Either suit would make a suitable trump suit.

3a) **2♠**. You have 3 HCPs plus 2 points for the six-card suit, for a total of 5 points. The partnership has from 21 to 23 combined points. The target level should be partscore. You have six spades, and partner has at least two, so there's an eight-card fit. As captain, put the partnership in partscore in spades.

3b) **4♥**. You have 10 HCPs plus 2 points for the six-card heart suit, for a total of 12 points. The combined partnership strength is at least 28 points, and at most 30 points. The target level should be game. There's an eight-card major suit fit, since you have six hearts, and partner has at least two. As captain, put the partnership in a game contract with hearts as the trump suit.

3c) **3NT**. You have 9 HCPs plus 1 point for the five-card diamond suit. That puts the combined partnership strength in the 26–28 point range, and the target should be the game level. There's no eight-card or longer fit in hearts or spades. Put the partnership in a game contract in notrump. Even if there's a minor suit fit, it's easier to try to take nine tricks in notrump rather than eleven tricks in clubs or diamonds.

Part 2

EVERYTHING YOU NEED TO KNOW ABOUT OPENING THE BIDDING

Opening the Bidding

"You can't judge the skill or intelligence of players by the range of their notrump bids."

It's the combined partnership strength and distribution that's important in determining a suitable contract. The challenge is to uncover these combined holdings using the language of bidding.

Think in terms of a bidding conversation rather than a single bid. As opener, you'll make an initial suggestion, and your partner will usually continue the conversation and respond. When it's your turn again, you'll choose a suitable rebid that tells partner more about your hand. Your partner may even bid again before the final destination is reached. You want to feel confident throughout the conversation. It all starts with the opening bid.

The Auction Begins

There are several considerations when you have the opportunity to bid. First, you need a reason to start the bidding. The value of a hand is a combination of the high cards and distribution. To open the bidding, you should have a better than average hand. Since the average number of HCPs in a hand is 10, better than average is generally accepted to be about 13 points, including distribution points. There are times when you may decide to open with a hand of 12 or fewer points. Your reason might be the size of the small cards—the tens and nines—or it might be the concentration of the high cards. Partner will assume that you have a better than average hand.

Having decided to open the bidding, the next consideration is the choice of opening bid. You can use the following guideline:

- With a balanced hand, and 16–18 points, open 1NT. Otherwise, open at the one level in your longest suit.

Let's take a closer look at these opening bids.

Opening 1NT

Opener wants to give as much information as quickly as possible. Your first consideration, if you have the values, is to start the bidding with 1NT. This is the bid that paints the most specific picture of your distribution and strength for partner.

Distribution

You need a balanced hand to open 1NT. Balanced refers to a hand with no voids, no singletons, and no more than one doubleton. Three hand patterns fall into this category:

X X X X	X X X X	X X X X X
X X X	X X X X	X X X
X X X	X X X	X X X
X X X	X X	X X
4–3–3–3	4–4–3–2	5–3–3–2

The numbers under each pattern refer to the cards in each suit. For example, 4–3–3–3 represent four cards in one suit, and three cards in each of the other suits. The order of the suits doesn't matter. For example, the hand could consist of three spades, three hearts, four diamonds, and three clubs.

Strength

The point count range for an opening notrump bid is narrow, usually a three–point range. A bid that shows such a limited range of strength is referred to as a limit bid. The most popular ranges in North America are 15–17 or 16–18 points. If you're playing with someone who has a British accent, however, don't be too surprised if your partner opens 1NT with 12–14 points—that's the fashionable style in England.

Count both high card points and length points when valuing your hand for an opening 1NT bid—a five-card suit is as valuable in a notrump contract as in a suit contract. The high cards can be distributed anywhere. It's no longer considered necessary to have high cards in your short suit when you have a doubleton. You might wonder what will happen if the opponents lead the suit. "You can't win them all," as the saying goes. An opening bid of 1NT is very specific and a good descriptive bid. Your bidding will be better if you use the bid as much as possible.

I'm often asked why bridge books aren't consistent about opening notrump bids. One book will suggest a range of 15–17 points, while another suggests a range of 16–18 or 12–14. Some books warn against opening 1NT with a worthless doubleton, or with a five-card major suit, or with all the high cards concentrated in two suits. Each of the variations has some merit, but there's no single "right" answer. Slight variations in style will continue to exist, so focus on the areas where there's a basic agreement.

The specific range your partnership selects is a matter of preference, not intelligence or skill. You certainly can't judge the competence of players by the range of their opening notrump bids. Which is better: one pinch or two pinches of salt in your stew? You wouldn't want to lose any friends over the answer. For the purpose of discussion throughout this book, a range of 16–18 points will be assumed.

In Search of the Best Opening Bid

Start the bidding 1NT if your hand meets the agreed requirements.

It gives your partner a clear picture of the shape and strength of your hand, and makes the subsequent auction much easier. Here are some examples.

♠ Q 10 8
♥ K Q 9 3
♦ A J 7
♣ K Q 4

This is the textbook 1NT opening bid. A balanced hand, with 17 points.

♠ A K J
♥ 9 8 5 4
♦ K Q 10 3
♣ A Q

The requirements for a 1NT opening bid are specific. Although this is a balanced hand, it's too strong to start with 1NT. There are 19 points. Instead, open the longest suit, 1♦.

♠ Q J 8 6
♥ A Q 9
♦ 3 2
♣ A Q J 4

Be confident about opening 1NT with this hand—yes, even with the worthless doubleton in diamonds.

♠ Q 9 4
♥ K 10 6
♦ A J
♣ K 9 7 6 3

With 13 HCPs plus 1 for the five-card club suit, this hand is worth only 14 points. Although it's balanced, it isn't strong enough to open the bidding 1NT. Instead, choose 1♣.

♠ K 10
♥ Q J 9
♦ A Q 9 7 3
♣ Q J 5

Value the five-card diamond suit as 1 point. Together with the 15 HCPs, there's ample strength to start with 1NT. This is much more descriptive than starting with 1♦.

♠ A 10 6 4
♥ K 7
♦ A 3
♣ K Q 7 6 4

There's enough strength to open the bidding 1NT, but the hand pattern isn't considered balanced. Instead, open in your longest suit, 1♣.

♠ K Q 9 6 3
♥ Q 10 7
♦ A Q 3
♣ K 5

Although this hand contains a five-card major suit, it should still be opened 1NT. The hand is balanced, and is worth 17 points.

Opening the Bidding One-of-a-Suit

If your hand doesn't meet the requirements for an opening bid of 1NT, but you have 13 or more points, open the bidding at the one level in your longest suit. For example:

♠ 10 5
♥ A J 9 8 3
♦ A J 10
♣ K 10 4

There are 13 HCPs plus 1 for the five-card heart suit. Open the bidding in the longest suit, 1♥.

Opening bids of 1♣, 1♦, 1♥, and 1♠ cover a much wider range of strength than 1NT. There's an upper limit to the range—about 21 points—yet opening bids of one-of-a-suit are not considered limit bids. The range is too wide.

Opening suit bids at the one level cover a broad range of hand patterns. They can be made on balanced hands, as in the above example, or on wildly distributional hands such as this:

♠ 4
♥ A Q 9 8 6 5
♦ 7
♣ K Q 10 6 4

With 11 HCPs plus 2 points for the six-card suit, and 1 point for the five-card suit, this hand would also be opened 1♥.

Opener will narrow the range of the strength and distribution of the hand as the auction progresses.

Length Before Strength

The best trump suit will usually be the one with the most cards in the combined partnership hands. To help partner decide on the best fit, start the bidding in the longest suit rather than the strongest. For example:

♠ A K Q 2
♥ 7 4
♦ J 9 8 7 5
♣ K 8

Open this hand 1♦ rather than 1♠. As the bidding progresses, you'll have an opportunity to uncover a spade fit, if there is one. If not, partner will be better placed to settle on the best contract with the knowledge that your longest suit is diamonds.

Suits of Equal Length

Sometimes you'll have a choice of suits. For example:

♠ K Q 8 6 2
♥ 10 9
♦ A Q J 9 3
♣ J

The next chapter will take a more detailed look at the guidelines for selecting suits depending on the partnership style. For now, use this straightforward approach:

• Open the higher-ranking of two suits of equal length.

On the above hand, open the bidding 1♠, since spades are higher-ranking than diamonds.

Open the bidding 1♦ with this hand, where you have a choice of four-card suits:

♠ A 8 3
♥ 7 5
♦ K Q 4 2
♣ A 10 8 4

Opening Bids in a Suit

♠ 8
♥ K 8 5
♦ K J 9 8 7 3
♣ A K J

This is an unbalanced hand with 15 HCPs plus 2 points for the six-card diamond suit. Open the longest suit, 1♦.

♠ Q J 9 2
♥ 10
♦ J 8 4
♣ A J 8 5 3

Pass. There are only 9 HCPs and 1 for the five-card club suit. That isn't enough strength to open the bidding at the one level.

♠ A J 10 8 5
♥ K 3
♦ 4
♣ K Q 9 6 2

Bid 1♠, the higher-ranking of the two five-card suits. Some players prefer to open 1♣ with this particular distribution, but 1♠ is equally popular, and is consistent with the guideline of opening the higher-ranking suit when you have a choice.

♠ A 4
♥ J 9 8 6 3
♦ A K 9 8 4
♣ 4

Open 1♥, the higher-ranking of the two five-card suits. The guideline says nothing about the relative strength of the suits.

♠ Q 9
♥ A J 7
♦ Q J 9 3 2
♣ K Q 10

Open 1NT. Opening 1NT always takes priority if you have an appropriate hand. This hand is balanced (5–3–3–2) with 15 HCPs plus 1 for the five-card diamond suit.

♠ K 10 7
♥ 3
♦ A Q J 3
♣ A K Q 10 4

Open 1♣, your longest suit. Opening bids at the one level cover a wide range of strength. This has 19 HCPs plus 1 for the five-card club suit. Partner won't know after your initial bid that your hand is much stronger than the 13 points needed

to open the bidding. You'll show your great strength at your next opportunity to bid. For now, you're only getting the ball rolling.

Two-Level Opening Bids in a Suit

Opening bids at the one level carry an invitational message. Partner
can choose to respond or to pass. There are times when your hand is
so strong that you don't want to give partner the option of passing.
For example:

> ♠ A K Q 10 8 5
> ♥ A K Q 9
> ♦ 3
> ♣ A Q

You have 24 HCPs, and 2 points for the six-card spade suit. That's
enough to make a game contract all by yourself, and it wouldn't take
too much strength in partner's hand for your side to make
a slam.

You could open the bidding with a very enthusiastic-sounding 1♠,
perhaps leaning over the table slightly, while smiling, and raising
your eyebrows. You want partner to get your message, "Don't pass,
we're on our way to a game or slam." At the moment of your gesture,
however, partner may be tying a shoelace or distracted in some other
way, and all may be lost. As it turns out, this is just as well. Gestures
and body language to convey your bidding message are not considered fair tactics in a bridge game, even in the friendliest of circles.

Hands too strong for an opening bid at the one level are opened
at the two level. The above hand would be opened 2♠, rather than
1♠. This is a forcing bid, rather than an invitational bid. Partner is
expected to respond, even with a hand of little or no strength.

The general range used for opening bids at the two level is 22 or
more points. This puts a ceiling of 21 points on opening bids at the
one level. There are different styles of opening two-bids in a suit,
and they will be discussed in a later chapter. For now, the following
guideline should suffice:

- With an unbalanced hand of 22 or more points, open at the two level in your longest suit. Bid the higher-ranking of equal-length suits.

For example:

♠ —
♥ A K J 10 9
♦ A 8 3
♣ A K Q 10 4

With an unbalanced hand of 21 HCPs plus 2 points for the two five-card suits, open the bidding 2♥, the higher-ranking suit.

Strong Balanced Hands

With strong balanced hands, the following guidelines can be used:

- With a balanced hand of 22–24 points, open 2NT.
- With a balanced hand of 25–27 points, open 3NT.

Unlike opening two-bids in a suit, these are invitational bids, since opener is describing a hand of limited strength. Here are some examples:

♠ A Q J
♥ A Q 8 3
♦ K J 7 5
♣ K Q

With a balanced hand of 22 HCPs, open 2NT.

♠ K J
♥ K Q J
♦ A Q 9
♣ A K Q 10 4

With a balanced hand of 25 HCPs plus 1 for the five-card suit, open 3NT.

Higher Level Opening Bids in a Suit

Since hands of 13–21 points are opened at the one level, and hands of 22 or more points are opened at the two level, the three level can be used for a different purpose. Opening bids in a suit at the three level show hands with less than the values for an opening bid, but with considerable playing strength based on a long suit. For example:

♠ 2
♥ K Q J 9 8 7 3
♦ 10 7 3
♣ 9 5

This hand doesn't meet the requirements for an opening bid at the one level, but will probably take six tricks if hearts is the trump suit. An opening bid of 3♥ shows this type of hand. It's called a preemptive opening bid, and a later chapter will discuss such bids in more detail.

Summary

The opening bidder starts the conversation for the partnership using the following guidelines:

- With less than 13 points, pass.
- With 13–21 points:
  - Open the bidding 1NT with a balanced hand, and 16–18 points.
  - Otherwise, open the bidding at the one level in your longest suit. With suits of equal length, bid the higher-ranking.
- With 22 or more points:
  - Open the bidding 2NT with a balanced hand, and 22–24 points.
  - Open the bidding 3NT with a balanced hand, and 25–27 points.
  - Otherwise, open the bidding at the two level in your longest suit. With suits of equal length, bid the higher-ranking.

Exercises

1. If you have the first opportunity to bid, what would you do with each of the following hands?

a) ♠ A 10 8 5
♥ K 8
♦ A Q 7 3
♣ Q J 4

b) ♠ A J 9 7 5 2
♥ 7 2
♦ Q 10 8
♣ A J

c) ♠ K 8
♥ 10 9 8 6 5
♦ A Q J 8
♣ K 5

d) ♠ J 5
♥ Q 7 3
♦ A 9 6 5 3
♣ Q 10 4

e) ♠ K J 8 5 3
♥ Q J 9
♦ A Q
♣ K 10 5

f) ♠ A K J
♥ Q 8
♦ K Q J 6
♣ K 10 8 4

g) ♠ –
♥ A J 8 6 5 3
♦ 3
♣ K Q J 7 5 4

h) ♠ A 10 6
♥ A Q 10
♦ K Q 9 8 4
♣ 7 3

i) ♠ K 9 4
♥ A J 6
♦ Q 10 7
♣ A 7 6 5

j) ♠ A K J 2
♥ Q J 7 3
♦ K Q J
♣ A Q

k) ♠ A 9 2
♥ A K J 4
♦ –
♣ A K Q J 8 3

l) ♠ A J 10
♥ A Q
♦ K Q J 10 8
♣ A K Q

Answers to Exercises

a) **1NT**. This is a balanced hand (4–4–3–2) with 16 HCPs.

b) **1♠**. There 12 HCPs plus 2 for the six-card suit. A total of 14 points. Open the bidding in your long suit.

c) **1♥**. The hand is worth 14 points—13 HCPs plus 1 point for the fifth heart. Open the longest suit. Length before strength.

d) **Pass**. With only 9 HCPS plus 1 for the five-card diamond suit, there's not enough strength to open the bidding at the one level.

e) **1NT**. Although there's a five-card major suit, this is still a balanced hand of 17 points—16 HCPs plus 1 for the five-card suit.

f) **1♦**. With 19 HCPs, the hand is too strong to open the bidding 1NT even though it's balanced. With a choice of four-card suits, open the higher-ranking, diamonds.

g) **1♥**. There are 11 HCPs plus 2 points for each of the six-card suits, for a total of 15 points. With a choice of six-card suits, open the higher-ranking, hearts.

h) **1NT**. Adding 1 point for the five-card diamond suit to the 15 HCPs makes this hand worth 16 points. A 5–3–3–2 pattern is balanced, so open 1NT. Don't worry about the small doubleton.

i) **1♣**. With a balanced hand, but only 14 HCPs, the hand isn't strong enough for an opening notrump bid. Instead, open the longest suit.

j) **2NT**. A balanced hand of 23 HCPs is opened at the two level in notrump.

k) **2♣**. A strong unbalanced hand of more than 21 points is opened at the two level, rather than the one level. This is a forcing bid, asking partner to bid, even with no points.

l) **3NT**. This is a balanced hand with 26 HCPs plus 1 for the five-card suit. An opening bid of 3NT is used to describe this type of hand to partner. Although it's a game contract, partner can bid more, knowing about opener's strength and distribution.

The Short Club,
Five-Card Majors—
and All That

*"And if you were playing five-card majors but forgot? If you
have to put down your hand as the dummy after the
auction is over, put one of your diamonds in with your
hearts. Partners are usually more sympathetic about poor
eyesight than poor memory!"*

A discussion of opening bids wouldn't be complete without considering two popular topics: the *short club* and *five-card majors*.

The Short Club

The practice of opening the bidding 1♣ with fewer than four cards
in the suit, instead of bidding your longest suit, is referred to as the
short club. One of the best tips I can give you about opening the bidding is this: don't cloud your thinking with concerns about the short

club. As soon as the "short" club becomes your focus, the bidding conversation can become uncomfortable.

One of my favorite authors, Edwin Kantar, a world champion, has this to say in a chapter headed "The Short Club Obsession":

> "Almost the first words uttered when two strangers sit down to play with one another are, 'Do you play the short club?' or 'I only open with a five-card major' or 'I play the short club, do you play the short diamond?' Help!"

So from now on, avoid starting your conversation with a new partner by saying, "Do you play the short club?" You won't miss the question, I assure you, and your partnership will be off to a more relaxed start. If your partner bids 1♣, assume that partner actually has a club suit. Yes, you could pass. 1♣ is not a forcing bid. Bill Root, another world champion and world-famous teacher, poses a problem with this hand:

♠ J 8 4
♥ 9 6 4 3 2
♦ 8 7 6 5
♣ 7

What do you do if your partner starts the bidding 1♣? Mr. Root's advice is simple:

> "Pass, before the roof caves in. Don't fear passing a 1♣ opening when you're short in clubs. If partner is left to play the 1♣ contract he will probably be set a few tricks for a small loss (although he may have a good club suit, and make it), while if you bid over 1♣ it may lead to a complete disaster."

There are occasions when you might open the bidding 1♣ with less than a four-card suit. To play better bridge, however, there are more important questions than whether or not partner plays the short club. One of them is: Do you play five-card majors?

Five-Card Major Suit Openings

There's a popular style of bidding which requires that opener have at least five cards in a major suit, either hearts or spades, to start by suggesting this suit as trump. This style is referred to as *five-card majors*. If your partnership style is to open the bidding 1♥ or 1♠ with only four cards in the suit, this is referred to as *four-card majors*.

There has been ongoing debate among the experts for a number of years over which is the better bidding method. In some countries, the Acol system is used. It's a four-card major system. In North America, the most popular bidding system is five-card majors, although world champions such as Bob Hamman still prefer four-card majors. Due to its popularity, five-card majors is the style I'm going to adopt throughout the book. On most hands, however, it will make little difference which method your partnership prefers.

Let's look at some examples. What would you open with the following hands?

♠ J 8
♥ K 10 8 7 6
♦ A Q 5
♣ K 9 4

1♥. This the natural opening bid on this hand, whether you play five-card or four-card majors.

♠ A K 10 4
♥ 9
♦ K J 9 6 4
♣ A 7 3

1♦. You still open your longest suit, whether you play four-card or five-card majors.

♠ A J 9 7 5
♥ K Q 8 4 3
♦ 5
♣ A Q

1♠. Open the higher-ranking of two five-card suits, whether you use four-card or five-card majors.

♠ A Q 9 6 2
♥ K J 8
♦ K 8
♣ Q J 7

1NT. The majority of bridge authorities, such as Bill Root, suggest that you open 1NT, even with a five-card major suit, when you have a balanced hand of appropriate strength. 1NT should take priority whenever possible.

♠ 8 7 6
♥ A K J 8
♦ A Q 8 5
♣ 10 4

1♦. Finally! Here's a hand which you could open 1♥ if you're using a four-card major style. Playing five-card majors, you can't open 1♥ without five cards in the suit. Instead, choose your minor suit, and open 1♦.

And if you were playing five-card majors but forgot? If you have to put down your hand as the dummy after the auction is over, put one of your diamonds in with your hearts. Partners are usually more sympathetic about poor eyesight than poor memory!

The Better Minor

Now we come to this type of hand:

♠ A 10 8 4
♥ K J 10 3
♦ 7 6
♣ K Q 4

You don't have a five-card major suit, but you do have enough strength to open the bidding. If you play five-card majors, you can't open 1♥ or 1♠. Instead you'll have to choose between clubs and diamonds. In this situation, bid your longer minor suit. This is sometimes referred to as the *better minor*. You would open the bidding 1♣, treating the club suit as though it were a four-card suit.

Although this is a "short" suit, and you hope that partner doesn't get carried away and agree on clubs as the trump suit, you shouldn't be concerned. As you'll see when we take a look at responding to opening bids, it's unlikely that clubs will end up as the trump suit unless partner has five or more of them. Even if partner passes your opening bid, playing in a contract of 1♣ will not be a disaster.

This is the type of hand that led to the coining of the phrase "short club." It really has little to do with shortness or clubs, it's merely a convenient way to start the auction when you can't bid a major suit.

Consider this hand:

> ♠ A 10 8 4
> ♥ K J 10 3
> ♦ K Q 4
> ♣ 7 6

Playing five-card majors, you would open this hand 1♦, your better minor suit. Nothing to do with clubs.

Here are more examples. Consider your opening bid on each of these hands, assuming you've agreed to play five-card majors:

♠ 5
♥ K 10 6 4
♦ A J 8 3
♣ K Q 7 3

1♦. You can't open 1♥ with only a four-card major suit, so choose between the minor suits. With a choice of four-card minor suits, the general style is to open the higher-ranking suit.

♠ K Q 6 3
♥ 4
♦ Q 8
♣ A Q 10 8 6 4

1♣. Open your long suit. This hand shows why you shouldn't worry if partner opens the bidding with 1♣ and you have to pass holding a singleton or doubleton club. Most of the time, the 1♣ opening bid will be perfectly natural, and clubs may be the best trump suit.

♠ Q J 8 3
♥ A Q 6 2
♦ K 5
♣ A J 6

1NT. Be careful. Remember not to focus on those three-card minor suits. This hand doesn't need to be opened 1♣. It falls beautifully into the range for a 1NT opening bid.

♠ Q 9 6 3
♥ A J 4
♦ K 10 8
♣ K J 5

1♣. You can't open 1♠ without a five-card suit, so you have to choose a minor suit. When choosing between two three-card minor suits of approximately equal strength, most players bid the lower-ranking—a small exception to the general guideline of opening the higher-ranking of two suits of equal length.

Summary

Using the style of five-card major opening bids, you can use the following guidelines for hands in the range of 13–21 points:

- Bid 1NT with a balanced hand and 16–18 points
- With a five-card or longer suit:
  - bid your longest suit.
  - bid the higher-ranking of two five-card or six-card suits.
- Otherwise:
  - bid your longer minor suit.
  - bid 1♦ with two four-card suits or 1♣ with two three-card suits.

Exercises

1. Assuming your partnership has agreed to play five-card majors, what would be your opening bid on each of the following hands? Would there be any difference if you are playing four-card majors?

a) ♠ A K 10 8 5
   ♥ 8
   ♦ K J 7 4
   ♣ Q 10 6

b) ♠ Q 10 8 6 2
   ♥ A K J 8 3
   ♦ 8 7
   ♣ A

c) ♠ 3
   ♥ A 10 9 8 6
   ♦ A Q J 9 6 3
   ♣ 4

d) ♠ A 6
   ♥ 8 7 6 5 3
   ♦ Q 7
   ♣ A K 8 2

e) ♠ Q 8 5
   ♥ Q J 9 6 2
   ♦ A Q J
   ♣ K J

f) ♠ A K J 6
   ♥ K 5 3
   ♦ Q J 8 6
   ♣ 10 7

g) ♠ 5
   ♥ K J 8 5
   ♦ A J 10 3
   ♣ A Q J 7

h) ♠ K 6
   ♥ A K 10 8
   ♦ J 9 2
   ♣ Q J 3 2

i) ♠ A Q 6 3
   ♥ K Q 6
   ♦ 10 7 2
   ♣ A K J

j) ♠ Q 9 7 6
   ♥ K 8 4 3
   ♦ K 6
   ♣ A Q 4

k) ♠ A 2
   ♥ A Q 10 5
   ♦ Q 3
   ♣ K Q J 7 4

l) ♠ A J 4
   ♥ A K Q 7
   ♦ 8 5 3
   ♣ 9 5 3

Answers to Exercises

a) **1♠.** With a five-card suit, open your long suit, whether you play four-card or five-card majors.

b) **1♠.** Open the higher-ranking of two five-card suits, whether playing four-card or five-card majors.

c) **1♦.** Open the longest suit, even with a five-card major. The same would be true playing four-card majors.

d) **1♥.** Playing either four-card or five-card majors, any five-card suit is biddable. It's the length, not the strength, that's important.

e) **1NT.** No matter what your bidding style, open 1NT when you have a balanced hand that falls into your opening notrump range.

f) **1♦.** Playing five-card majors, you can't open 1♠ with only a four-card suit. Open your longer minor instead. Playing four-card majors, you could open this hand 1♠.

g) **1♦.** Playing five-card majors you open the higher-ranking of your two four-card minor suits when you can't open a major suit. Those playing four-card majors would probably also open 1♦, the middle-ranking of the three four-card suits, although some players might prefer to open 1♥.

h) **1♣.** Open your longer minor with no five-card major. This hand would be opened 1♥ if your partnership style is four-card majors.

i) **1♣.** This hand is too strong to open with 1NT and there's no five-card major. With a choice between the three-card minors, open 1♣. Those playing four-card majors would open this hand 1♠.

j) **1♣.** Even with two four-card major suits, open the bidding in your longest minor suit if you play five-card majors. Those playing four-card majors might open this hand 1♥—lower-ranking of two four-card suits—or 1♠—higher-ranking of two four-card suits—but might also open the bidding 1♣ with such poor major suits.

k) **1♣.** This would be the opening bid playing either four-card or five-card majors, since clubs is the longest suit in the hand. 1♣ is a perfectly natural bid on this hand. Partner shouldn't assume that it's a "short" suit.

1)   1♣. Adhering strictly to five-card majors, this hand is opened in the "better" minor suit. This is the type of hand that favors those playing four-card majors. Even staunch five-card major advocates might prefer to open this hand 1♥, treating their strong hearts as five-card suit—or hoping partner won't notice.

Part 3

BEING
COMFORTABLE
WITH YOUR
FIRST RESPONSE

Responding to an Opening Bid of 1NT

*"On any given hand, the cards and the bidding,
not the personality of the players, determine which
player is the captain."*

The responses to an opening bid of 1NT are important not only in themselves, but because they provide a blueprint for the whole bidding process.

The opening bid of 1NT is referred to as a limit bid. It puts a narrow limit on both the strength and distribution of the opening bidder's hand. The value of opener's hand lies within a three-point range. A range of 16, 17 or 18 points is used for an opening bid of 1NT in the examples throughout this book. Opener has also shown a balanced hand, with no voids or singletons, and at most one doubleton. Responder can often make a final decision about the contract right away because so much information is exchanged through this one bid.

Responder's Bidding Messages

The responder after a 1NT opening bid can make use of all three bidding messages.

Sometimes responder wants to make a sign-off bid—a "stop" or "red" bid—telling opener to pass. After all, responder knows about opener's distribution, and knows the maximum value of opener's hand. Opener knows nothing about responder's hand. In this situation, responder plays the role of captain, placing the contract.

Responder may need to send an invitational message—a "proceed with caution" or "yellow" bid—if more information is needed about opener's exact strength to help decide whether to go for a game or slam bonus.

There are times when responder needs to make a forcing bid—a "go" or "green" bid—to get more information about opener's distribution before making a decision on the contract.

Responder uses the bidding messages in various situations:

- When responder knows the target is a game contract.
- When responder knows the target is a partscore contract.
- When responder is uncertain about the target.

Responding to 1NT
When the Target Is Game

When I'm lecturing on responses to 1NT, I often have the audience hold up both hands and wiggle their fingers and their thumbs to represent the number ten. What's so special about this number? If responder has at least 10 points, it's the responder's job to get the partnership to game. Opener is showing at least 16 points, and 16 + 10 = 26, the number of points required to have a good chance of being successful at the game level.

The maximum strength opener is showing is 18 points. Unless responder has 15 or more points, there isn't enough combined strength to bid a slam contract. So, in the 10–14 point range, responder's target is a game contract, usually 3NT, 4♥, or 4♠.

Responder knows a lot about opener's distribution, and can often place the partnership in a game contract right away. Since responder is acting as captain in this situation, responder's jumps to game are sign-off bids. Opener is expected to pass. Here are some examples for responder:

♠ K 10 3
♥ Q 6 4
♦ A 10 8 2
♣ J 9 3

3NT. Responder has 10 HCPs, enough to know that the partnership belongs in a game contract. With no particular interest in the major suits, the best place to play the hand is in notrump. Responder jumps directly to 3NT. This is a sign-off bid. Responder has chosen the game, and opener should pass.

♠ J 4
♥ K 9 4
♦ A Q 8 6 3
♣ 10 8 7

3NT. Responder has 10 HCPs plus 1 for the five-card suit, a total of 11 points. The partnership may have an eight-card or longer fit in diamonds, but the partnership is unlikely to have enough strength to make a 5♦ contract. You would need to take eleven tricks in a 5♦ contract, but you need only nine tricks in a 3NT contract. Go for the easier game bonus.

♠ Q 7
♥ J 6
♦ Q 9 5
♣ K J 10 8 4 2

3NT. This is a more extreme example of avoiding playing in a minor suit when you're likely to be able to take nine tricks in a notrump contract. To have a balanced hand, partner must have at least two clubs. So, there's an eight-card or longer fit. It's more likely, however, that you can take nine tricks in notrump than eleven tricks with clubs as trump.

♠ Q J 8 7 6 4
♥ 9 4
♦ A J 5
♣ K 4

4♠. The situation is different when you have an eight-card major suit fit. Partner must have at least two spades, and could have more. Playing in a major suit fit is preferable to playing in notrump. Bid game in the major suit. This is a sign-off bid. You have not asked opener for any further information. As captain, you know where the partnership belongs.

There's no need on any of the above hands to bid less than a game contract. You have all the information you need to make a good decision and can assume the role of captain. There's no value in asking your partner for further information when you already have all the information you need. But consider this hand:

    ♠ 10 7
    ♥ K Q 9 8 5
    ♦ A 10 8 3
    ♣ Q 6

With 11 HCPs plus 1 for the five-card suit, you know that the partnership should play in a game contract. You're not sure, however, which game contract would be best. If partner has three or four hearts, you have a major suit fit, and belong in a 4♥ contract. If partner has only two hearts, there's no major suit fit, and 3NT should be the best contract.

The way responder finds out the additional information required to make an appropriate decision is by making a forcing bid to which opener must reply. Responder jumps to 3♥. This is a forcing response, asking opener to choose between 3NT and 4♥. With only two hearts, opener is expected to bid 3NT; with three or more hearts, opener goes on to 4♥.

It's important that the 1NT opener realizes that a jump response of 3♥, or 3♠, is a forcing bid. This is part of the language of bidding. Once opener recognizes the response as a forcing bid, the decision to carry on to 3NT or game in the major suit comes naturally.

With a six-card major suit, responder jumps right to game in the suit, as a sign-off bid. With a five-card major suit, responder jumps to the three level, as a forcing bid, asking opener to choose between 3NT and game in the major suit. What if responder has only a four-card major suit?

    ♠ K J 6 3
    ♥ 7 4
    ♦ K 10 8 3
    ♣ A 7 4

Later in this book, you'll be introduced to the Stayman Convention which is an *artificial* response of 2♣ designed to find out if opener has a four-card major suit. Until you reach that point, you could simply raise to 3NT with the above hand. That's likely to be a reasonable game contract. If partner has four spades—we'll meet that challenge later!

Responding to 1NT
When the Target Is Partscore

With 7 or fewer points, responder knows that the partnership belongs in a partscore contract. The 1NT opening bid was limited to a maximum of 18 points. The combined partnership strength must be less than the 26 points ordinarily needed to make a game contract. So, with 0–7 points, responder's target is the best partscore contract.

After 1NT there isn't much room left for responder to find out any further information about opener's hand. Responder must act as captain and settle on a suitable contract. With a five-card or longer suit, responder bids the suit at the two level. This is a sign-off bid, and opener is expected to pass. Without a five-card suit, responder simply passes, leaving opener to play in 1NT. For example:

♠ 10 8 3	Pass. With only 4 HCPs, the partnership
♥ Q 7 3	belongs in partscore, since opener has at most
♦ J 8 5 2	18 points. With no five-card or longer suit, re-
♣ J 10 6	sponder passes, leaving the partnership in a
	partscore contract of 1NT.

♠ Q 10 8 6 5 4	2♠. There are 3 HCPs plus 2 points for the
♥ 7 3	six-card suit. With only 5 points, responder
♦ J 8 3	knows the partnership has at most 23 combined
♣ 9 4	points (5 + 18 = 23), and could have as few as 21
	(5 + 16 = 21). Responder must pick the best

partscore. Opener's balanced hand must contain at least two spades, so there's an eight-card or longer fit. Responder places the contract in a partscore of 2♠. This is a sign-off bid, and opener is expected to pass.

♠ 7 3
♥ K 10 8 6 4
♦ Q 9 5 2
♣ 6 3

2♥. 5 HCPs plus 1 for the five-card suit adds up to 6 points, not enough for responder to consider a game contract. The best partscore contract is likely to be 2♥. Opener may have only two hearts, but responder has no bidding room left to find out. It's reasonable to assume that opener has three or more hearts, and there's an eight-card fit. If it turns out that opener has a doubleton, 2♥ should still be a reasonable contract.

♠ 10 3
♥ J 6 4
♦ 8 6 3
♣ Q J 7 4 2

Pass. Although responder normally makes a sign-off at the two level with a five-card or longer suit, the response of 2♣ is reserved for the Stayman Convention, which will be discussed in a subsequent chapter. For now, pass if you have a weak hand with clubs as your only long suit. We'll see later on how to get to play a partscore contract in clubs.

Responding to 1NT
When Responder Is Uncertain of the Target

When responder has 8 or 9 points, a sign-off bid is not appropriate. Opener may have 18 points, and the partnership total would be 26 or 27 points, enough for a game contract. On the other hand, responder can't commit the partnership to a game contract, since opener may have only 16 points, and the partnership would hold 24 or 25 points, not quite enough strength for game.

When responder doesn't have enough information about opener's strength to make a final decision on the contract, responder can make an invitational bid asking opener's opinion on whether or not the partnership should go higher. Responder can do this by bidding 2NT.* For example:

---

* With 8 or 9 points, and interest in playing in a major suit, responder needs to use the Stayman Convention. More on that later.

♠ Q 3
♥ J 10 7
♦ K 9 6 4
♣ K 8 4 2

Responder has 9 HCPs. This is too much to pass, but not enough to jump to 3NT. Responder compromises by bidding 2NT, an invitational bid.

The auction will now go back to opener. The opening bid of 1NT got the bidding conversation started. Responder didn't have enough information to place the contract. Now, following responder's invitational bid, opener must decide the fate of the hand. With the bottom of the promised range of strength, 16 points, opener should pass, declining the invitation. With the top of the range, 18 points, opener should accept, and carry on to 3NT. With the middle of the 1NT range, 17 points, opener can bid or pass. I suggest that you consider this as being in the upper part of the range, and carry on to game.

Slam Decisions

When responder holds more than 14 points, there's the possibility of a slam contract. Approximately 33 combined points are needed for a small slam, and 37 points are needed for a grand slam. Slam bidding will be looked at more closely in a future chapter. For now, responder can apply similar principles to those used for inviting or bidding game contracts when thinking about a slam contract. For example, consider the following hands after partner has opened the bidding 1NT:

♠ A 10 6
♥ K J 5
♦ Q J 8
♣ A Q 9 3

6NT. Responder has 17 HCPs. Opener has at least 16 points, and at most 18 points. The partnership holds between 33 and 35 points. That's enough for a small slam, and responder, as captain, can put the partnership in the best contract of 6NT. Like the response of 3NT, a raise to 6NT is a sign-off bid. Opener is expected to pass.

♠ –
♥ A J 10 8 6 4 2
♦ A J 3
♣ K J 5

6♥. There are 14 HCPs plus 3 for the seven-card heart suit. The partnership must have at least 33 combined points. Since opener must hold at least two hearts to have a balanced hand, the partnership has a nine-card or longer major suit fit. Responder can jump directly to a slam contract. As we shall see later on, there are other methods for bidding to a slam contract, but 6♥ should prove a practical bid on this hand.

♠ A Q 3
♥ K Q 5
♦ K J 10 4
♣ A K 8

7NT. With 22 HCPs, the combined hands could contain all 40 HCPs in the deck. There are at least 38 combined points, so responder can confidently commit the partnership to taking all the tricks. There should be a little excitement at the table when this hand is bid!

♠ K J 6
♥ Q 10 7
♦ A K 8
♣ Q J 5 2

4NT. Like the raise to 2NT, inviting opener to carry on to game with 17 or 18 points, a raise to 4NT—one level beyond game—invites opener to carry on to slam. On this hand, responder has 16 points. If opener has 17 or 18 points, there should be enough combined strength for slam. With only 16 points, opener will reject the invitation by passing, and the partnership remains at a safe level, having explored for the possibility of slam.

The raise to 4NT in this situation is referred to as a *quantitative* or *invitational raise*. It shouldn't be confused with the Blackwood Convention which is an artificial, forcing bid that will be discussed in the chapter on slam bidding.

Summary

When partner opens the bidding 1NT (16–18 points), use the following guidelines as responder:

0–7 points	Bid 2♦, 2♥, or 2♠ with a five-card or longer suit. These are sign-off bids. (2♣ is reserved for the Stayman Convention.) Otherwise, pass.
8–9 points	Bid 2NT. This is an invitational bid. (The Stayman Convention can be used when responder is interested in a major suit.)
10–14 points	Bid 4♥ or 4♠ with a six-card or longer suit. These are sign-off bids.
	Bid 3♥ or 3♠ with a five-card suit. These are forcing bids.
	Otherwise, bid 3NT. This is a sign-off bid. (The Stayman Convention can be used when responder is interested in a four-card major suit.)
15–16 points	Invite opener to a slam contract.
17 or more	Bid to a slam contract.

Exercises

1. What message is responder sending opener with the following responses to 1NT?

a) 2♥   b) 3♥   c) 4♥

d) 2NT   e) 3NT   f) 4NT

2. What would you respond to an opening bid of 1NT with each of the following hands?

a) ♠ 6 3
   ♥ K 8 5 3
   ♦ J 10 6 4
   ♣ J 9 4

b) ♠ 8 3
   ♥ J 9 7 6 5 3
   ♦ 10 7
   ♣ J 8 4

c) ♠ K Q 10 8 3 2
   ♥ A 6 4
   ♦ 3
   ♣ J 7 2

d) ♠ Q 5
   ♥ J 8 3
   ♦ A K 10 8 3
   ♣ Q 10 7

e) ♠ K 9 7
   ♥ J 5
   ♦ A J 6 3
   ♣ 9 7 6 3

f) ♠ 7 5
   ♥ Q J 9 8 3
   ♦ 6 2
   ♣ A K 10 6

g) ♠ 7
   ♥ 10 8 3
   ♦ Q J 2
   ♣ A Q 9 7 5 4

h) ♠ Q 10 7 4 3
   ♥ 10 5
   ♦ K 8 4 3 2
   ♣ 6

i) ♠ J 7 4 2
   ♥ 6
   ♦ Q 9 8 3
   ♣ J 8 6 2

j) ♠ 10 9 2
   ♥ K 3
   ♦ K J 10 8 6 3
   ♣ 8 4

k) ♠ Q 4
   ♥ J 5
   ♦ 10 8 6 3
   ♣ K 10 8 4 3

l) ♠ K Q
   ♥ Q J 5
   ♦ A J 8 6
   ♣ K J 9 3

3. You open 1NT with the following hand:

♠ K J 8   What do you bid if partner bids:
♥ J 4
♦ A Q 8 6   a) 2♥?   b) 3♥?   c) 2NT?   d) 3♠?
♣ A J 5 4

Answers to Exercises

1a) Sign-off. Responder wants to play a partscore of 2♥.

1b) Forcing. Responder is asking opener to choose between 3NT and 4♥.

1c) Sign-off. Responder wants to play a game contract of 4♥.

1d) Invitational. Responder wants opener to bid game with 17 or 18 points, otherwise pass.

1e) Sign-off. Responder wants to play a game contract of 3NT.

1f) Invitational. Responder wants opener to bid slam with 17 or 18 points, otherwise pass.

2a) Pass. With 5 HCPs there isn't enough for a game. Leave opener in the best partscore contract.

2b) 2♥. With 2 HCPs plus 2 points for the six-card heart suit, play in the best partscore. 2♥ is a sign-off bid.

2c) 4♠. With 10 HCPs and 2 points for the six-card suit, the partnership belongs in a game contract. Since opener is balanced, the partnership has at least an eight-card spade fit.

2d) 3NT. With 1 point for the five-card diamond suit and 12 HCPs, there's enough for game. 3NT should be easier to make than 5♦, even if there's a diamond fit.

2e) 2NT. With 9 HCPs, invite opener to bid game with the top range of the 1NT opening. With only 16 points, opener will pass.

2f) 3♥. With 10 HCPs plus a five-card suit the partnership belongs in game. 3♥ asks opener to choose between 3NT and 4♥.

2g) 3NT. There are 9 HCPs plus 2 points for the six-card club suit. The partnership belongs in game, and 3NT requires only 9 tricks. There's unlikely to be enough combined strength to make 11 tricks in a 5♣ contract. Don't worry about the singleton spade; partner is likely to have some high cards in the suit.

2h) 2♠. With only 5 HCPs and 1 point for each of the five-card suits, there isn't enough for game. With a choice of five-card suits, bid the higher-ranking, as when opening the bidding.

2i) **Pass.** There are only 4 HCPs. Although the hand contains a singleton, there's no five-card suit to bid. Pass and hope for the best.

2j) **2NT.** 7 HCPs plus 2 points for the six-card diamond suit is enough to invite opener to game. Opener will pass with a minimum-strength hand and bid 3NT with the top of the range.

2k) **Pass.** With only 6 HCPs plus 1 for the five-card suit, the partnership belongs in partscore. Although there's a five-card club suit, a response of 2♣ is not (normally) used as a sign-off bid. Pass, and leave opener to play partscore in 1NT.

2l) **6NT.** With 17 HCPs, the combined partnership assets are between 33 and 35 points. 33 points is enough for a small slam contract.

3a) **Pass.** 2♥ is a sign-off bid by responder.

3b) **3NT.** 3♥ is a forcing response asking opener to choose between 3NT and 4♥. With only a doubleton heart, choose 3NT.

3c) **Pass.** 2NT is an invitational bid. With only 16 HCPs, the bottom of the notrump range, decline the invitation and settle for partscore.

3d) **4♠.** 3♠ is forcing, asking opener to choose between 3NT and 4♠. With three-card support for partner's five-card spade suit, choose 4♠ since there's an eight-card major suit fit.

♣ ♦ ♥ ♠ ♣ ♦ ♥ ♠ ♣ ♦ ♥ ♠ **6** ♣ ♦ ♥ ♠ ♣ ♦ ♥ ♠ ♣ ♦ ♥ ♠ ♣

Responding to an Opening Bid of 1♥ or 1♠

"If you find you have three opponents at the bridge table, put an ad in the newspaper for a new bridge partner."

Responder takes over, so to speak, after the limited opening bid of 1NT. Responder often has enough information to place the contract right away, and assumes the role of captain. There are several bids that responder can make which are sign-off bids asking opener to pass.

When the opening bid is at the one level in a major suit, either 1♥ or 1♠, responder is no longer able to make a quick decision about the contract. Opener hasn't limited the hand to a narrow range of strength. Opener could have anywhere from a very minimum-strength hand of 13 points up to a very strong hand of 21 points—not quite enough to open with a forcing bid at the two level. In addition, opener can have a variety of hand patterns. Opener's hand could be balanced, semi-balanced or very unbalanced.

As responder to an opening bid of one-of-a-major, you're not in a position to make a sign-off bid asking opener to pass. You don't know enough about opener's hand. Start off by making either an invitational or forcing bid to get more information from opener. Opener can then make a further description of the hand, and the partnership will be well placed to settle on a contract.

There are variations that can be incorporated in responses to major suits. I prefer to keep the bidding as natural as possible, doing what comes instinctively. You have only four choices after a major suit opening:

- Passing.
- Supporting partner's suit.
- Bidding a suit of your own.
- Bidding notrump.

Time to Pass

Partner opens the bidding 1♠, and this is your hand:

♠ 9 8 7 4
♥ J 4 3
♦ Q 6 2
♣ 9 5 4

Good! Partner likes spades and you have four. You're pleased with partner's suggestion that spades would make a good trump suit. Even if partner is at the top of the range for an opening bid at the one level, the game target is too ambitious. Pass, and leave partner to play in a partscore of 1♠. Even if you have as many as 5 points, it's unlikely that the partnership belongs in a game contract. After all, partner could have as few as 13 points. The general guideline is:

- With 0–5 points, pass when partner opens the bidding 1♥ or 1♠.

Agreeing with Partner

A trump contract will usually be better than a notrump contract if the partnership has an eight-card or longer fit. This is especially true if there's a fit in a major suit. One of the first priorities of the partnership is to try to agree on a major suit. Once that has been done, it's only a matter of deciding on the target level: partscore, game, or slam.

Trump Support

Partner starts the bidding 1♠, showing a five-card or longer suit and 13–21 points, and you hold this hand:

♠ Q 10 6
♥ 9 4
♦ K 8 5 2
♣ Q 9 6 3

You have three spades, and partner has five or more; the partnership has an eight-card major suit fit. You can agree with partner that spades would be a good trump suit. You have *adequate trump support*. Plan to *raise*, or *support*, partner's suit. The partnership can now settle on the appropriate level based on the combined strength of the hands.

Revaluation

Hand value can rise or fall as the auction unfolds. Consider this hand:

♠ 10 7 5 3
♥ –
♦ K 9 7 5 4
♣ A Q 7 3

You would initially value it as 10 points—9 HCPs plus 1 for the five-card diamond suit. If partner were to open the bidding 1♠, you have good support for spades and plan to raise partner's suit. The void in the heart suit should be an asset. If the opponents were to lead the ♥A, your side can play a small spade, a trump, and win the trick. The void is at least as valuable as an ace. It may be more valuable because it could prevent the opponents from taking any tricks in the suit, even if they hold the ♥A–K–Q.

Revalue your hand's distribution by giving yourself 5 points for the void, rather than 1 point for the five-card diamond suit. These are called *dummy points*, since you're planning to put the hand down as the dummy with partner playing in the agreed trump suit. Your hand would now be worth 14 points—9 HCPs plus 5 dummy points for the heart void.

The heart void is valuable only because you're planning to agree on spades as the trump suit. If partner were to start the bidding 1♥, it would be a different story. Now the void in hearts becomes a potential liability. You would continue to value the hand as 10 points.

A singleton or doubleton can also be useful when you have good support for partner's trump suit. The following scale of dummy points can be used when planning to raise partner's major suit:

Dummy Points

Void	5 points
Singleton	3 points
Doubleton	1 points

For example, consider the following hands after partner opens the bidding 1♠.

♠ J 8 6 3
♥ Q 9 7 3
♦ 4
♣ K J 8 2

With good support for partner's suit, you plan to raise. Revalue the hand using dummy points. You have 7 HCPs plus 3 for the singleton diamond, a total of 10 points.

♠ K Q 7 4
♥ Q J 4
♦ A 8 6 3
♣ 7 3

There are 12 HCPs. Add 1 point for the doubleton club, bringing the hand up to 13 points in support of partner's spade suit.

Finding the Target

Once you've decided to support partner's major, and have revalued your hand using dummy points, you want to communicate two things: your agreement to play in partner's suggested major suit, and the approximate strength of your hand. Knowing there's a trump fit and the combined strength of the two hands, partner can then judge the appropriate level for the contract. Remember, partner can have anywhere from 13 to 21 points for the opening bid.

There's not enough bidding room available for responder to show the exact strength of the hand, so responder usually tries to communicate one of the following three ranges:

- I like your suit, and have about 6–10 points (minimum raise).
- I like your suit, and have about 11–12 points (medium raise).
- I like your suit, and have 13 or more points (maximum raise).

There are a number of ways that this information can be conveyed to partner. A number of years ago, I wrote a book called *The Joy of Bridge* with world champion Eric Rodwell, and we adopted the most straightforward approach: the more responder has, the more responder bids. With 6–10 points, responder raises to the two level; with 11–12 points, responder raises to the three level; with 13–16 points, responder raises to the four level; and so on. This very practical approach is similar to the English ACOL system.

In North America and some other places around the world, however, many bridge players prefer to use the immediate raise to the game level as a *preemptive raise* showing excellent trump support, but very little strength outside of the trump suit. For example, if partner opens 1♥, you might respond 4♥ with a hand like this:

♠ 10 3
♥ Q 9 8 6 3
♦ 4
♣ K 10 8 6 2

This is a departure from the guideline of needing 26 or more points for a game contract, but it's a two-way adventure. First, partner might have the extra strength necessary to make the 4♥ contract, and when the partnership holds ten trumps, it can often make a lot of tricks with fewer than 26 combined points. Second, even if your side can't make 4♥ the opponents might be able to make a high-level contract, and the jump to 4♥ leaves them little room to exchange information.

Whatever the merits of using the raise to the four level in this manner, it does create a challenge for responder to show three different ranges of strength with only two levels now available for raising partner's suit: a raise to the two level, and a raise to the three level.

A raise of opener's major to the two level is commonly used to show responder's minimum range of strength:

OPENER		RESPONDER
1♠	*(I have 13 or more points and am suggesting spades as the trump suit)*	2♠ *(I have adequate trump support and 6–10points)*

After this, the paths diverge. One approach is to use the jump raise to the three level to show good trump support, and 13 or more points. Since opener has also promised 13 points, this bid is a *forcing raise*. Opener must bid again, since the partnership is known to have 26 or more combined points. What does responder do with the medium-range hand of 11–12 points? Responder starts by bidding a new suit, planning to show the support for opener's suit by bidding it at the three level the next time around.

Another approach is to use the jump raise to the three level to show good trump support, and 11–12 points. This is an invitational rather, rather than a forcing raise, and opener can pass with only 13 or 14 points. Since it limits responder's hand to 11–12 points, it's referred to as a *limit raise*. Playing this style, what does responder do holding 13 or more points with support for opener's suit? There are some conventional methods that can be used, but the more natural method is to start by bidding a new suit, planning to show support for opener's suit by bidding it at the game level the next time around.

Let's look at some sample hands, and see how they would be bid using both the "forcing raise", and "limit raise" approaches. Partner opens the bidding 1♥.

♠ K 4
♥ J 8 3
♦ 10 8 6 5
♣ A 7 5 3

2♥. With 8 HCPs, and three-card support for hearts, you have enough to raise partner's suit to the two level. Both approaches would result in a response of 2♥ with this hand.

♠ 9 4 3
♥ Q J 8 5
♦ K 4
♣ A J 8 6

The hand falls into the 11–12 point range. If you play forcing raises, this hand is too strong for a raise to 2♥, but not strong enough for a raise to 3♥ which would show 13 or more points. Instead, you would start by bidding a new suit, 2♣, intending to bid 3♥ at your next opportunity. This hand is easier if you play limit raises because you can jump to 3♥ right away, showing an invitational raise with 11–12 points.

♠ 8
♥ K J 8 3
♦ A Q 10 8 4
♣ Q 6 2

This hand has 12 HCPs, and you can add 3 points for the singleton spade, since you like partner's spades and you expect your hand to be the dummy. That gives you a total of 15 points. Playing forcing raises, you can jump directly to 3♥, forcing, showing 13 or more points, and good trump support. Playing limit raises, you can't bid 3♥ because it would show only 11–12 points, and opener might pass. Instead, you would bid 2♦, a new suit, planning to jump to 4♥ at your next bid to show that you would really like to play the hand in game with hearts as the trump suit.

As you can see, both forcing and limit raises have advantages on some hands, but disadvantages on others. Your partnership should choose the style with which it's most comfortable—perhaps even the *Joy of Bridge* approach. For consistency, the limit raise approach will be used for the remainder of this book.

Responder Bids a New Suit

If you can't raise partner's suit right away, but have a hand that's too strong to pass, you have two choices: you can bid a new suit or bid notrump. If possible, you want to bid a new suit, since the partnership is still searching for a suitable trump fit. A response in a new suit is unlimited, and can be done on any hand of 6 or more points. Because it's unlimited, it's a forcing bid, and opener is expected to bid again.

Looking for a trump suit is important, but you can't afford to get the partnership too high when you have a responding hand of minimum strength, about 6–10 points. If you have to move to the two level to bid a new suit, you should generally have about 11 or more points. Let's look at some examples after partner has opened the bidding 1♥.

♠ Q J 8 7
♥ 8 4
♦ Q J 3
♣ 10 8 7 3

1♠. There are only 6 HCPs, but you shouldn't pass. Partner might have a very strong hand of about 20 points, and you could miss a game contract. With only two cards in hearts, you can't support partner's major suit.

Instead, mention your four-card spade suit, since you can bid a new suit at the one level with 6 or more points. The requirement for having a five-card major suit to open the bidding 1♥, or 1♠, doesn't apply when responding to the opening bid. You can bid any four-card or longer suit. This is how you would find an eight-card spade fit if both you and opener hold four cards in the suit.

♠ A Q J 8 6 3
♥ 7
♦ K Q 10
♣ A 8 4

1♠. This time you have 16 HCPs plus 2 points for the six-card suit. You'll still respond only 1♠, even though there's enough combined strength for the partnership to play in a game contract. Before deciding on the game contract, however, you need more information about the combined hands. The response of 1♠ is unlimited, and forcing. Opener will bid again, and you'll be in a better position to judge whether the contract should be played in a trump suit or in notrump.

♠ 6 3
♥ J 7
♦ K 10 7
♣ A Q J 8 6 2

2♣. There are 11 HCPs plus 2 points for the six-card suit. You can't support partner's suit, but you have enough strength to introduce a new suit at the two level. You need about 11 or more points to bid a new suit at the two level, since you haven't yet agreed on a trump suit. Opener is forced to bid again, even on minimum values for the opening bid.

♠ J 3
♥ 9 2
♦ K Q 8 3
♣ A K 10 7 5

2♣. With a choice of suits that you can show, bid the longer suit first. There are 13 HCPs plus 1 for the five-card suit. That's enough to bid a new suit at the two level. With a choice between clubs and diamonds, bid the longer suit.

♠ A 3
♥ 7
♦ K J 10 7 5
♣ A Q 9 8 3

2♦. With a choice between two five-card or six-card suits, bid the higher-ranking. This hand is worth 14 HCPs plus 1 point for each of the five-card suits, more than enough to bid a new suit at the two level. With a choice of five-card suits, bid the higher-ranking, diamonds.

Although you may have two suits to show, you may not always have a choice about which to bid due to the constraint of needing 11 or more points to bid a new suit at the two level. For example:

♠ Q 10 8 3
♥ 6 5
♦ 10 4
♣ A J 10 7 2

1♠. Although the club suit is longer than the spade suit, the hand isn't strong enough to bid a new suit at the two level. Instead, you can show the spade suit at the one level, since that can be done on 6 or more points.

Responding in Notrump

The mere mention of notrump brings forth a vision of balanced hands, and narrow point ranges. As in other games, however, the opening move does not always follow the same pattern as the moves during the game. Consider a tennis game. The initial serve must go into a narrow boundary to be acceptable. Once the ball is in play, the boundaries are wider, and the players hit it all over the court.

The 1NT Response

The requirements for an opening notrump bid lie within a narrow range. An opening bid of 1NT shows a balanced hand with 16–18 points. Once the ball is in play, the range varies. To respond 1NT, all you need is a hand of 6–10 points with which you can't support partner's suit or bid a new suit at the one level. The hand doesn't need to be balanced. It's used for a variety of hands that fall into the 6–10 point range. Here are some typical hands that would fall into this category after partner opens the bidding 1♠.

♠ 7 3
♥ K 9 8 7
♦ J 10 7
♣ Q J 8 3

1NT. You don't have support for partner's spade suit, but the hand contains 7 HCPs, too much to pass. There are two suits you might want to mention, hearts and clubs, but neither of them can be bid at the one level, and you need 11 or more points to bid a new suit at the two level. The only response left is 1NT.

♠ 5
♥ K 8
♦ Q J 9 7 5 2
♣ J 8 4 3

1NT. Although the hand is unbalanced, you can't mention the six-card diamond suit because the hand is worth only 9 points—7 HCPs plus 2 for the six-card suit. You need 11 or more points to introduce a new suit at the two level.

The 1NT bid limits responder's hand to 6–10 points, and is an invitational bid. Opener can pass if 1NT appears to be the best contract or can bid again in search of a better contract. On the above hand, you might end up playing in a contract of 1NT, or you might get an opportunity to mention your diamond suit later in the auction now that you've limited your hand to the 6–10 point range.

The 2NT and 3NT Responses

Technically, there's no need to use a response of 2NT, or 3NT. With 11 or more points, you'll always be able to either raise partner's suit or bid a new suit of your own, even if it has to be bid at the two level. For this reason, the responses of 2NT and 3NT are sometimes given artificial meanings by the partnership, especially in response to a major suit. 2NT, for example, is often used to show the forcing raise of opener's major suit—13 or more points, and good trump support—by those who use the limit raise approach.

Nonetheless, some partnerships prefer to give a natural meaning to the responses of 2NT and 3NT. There are two common styles, similar to the two styles of forcing or limit raises. First, the forcing approach:

2NT   13–15 points, and a balanced hand without good support for opener's major suit. This is a forcing bid.

3NT   16–18 points, and a balanced hand without good support for opener's major suit.

The limit approach gives the following meanings to the responses:

2NT   11–12 points, and a balanced hand without good support for opener's major suit. This is an invitational bid.

3NT   13–15 points, and a balanced hand without good support for opener's major suit.

For example, consider the following hand after an opening bid of 1♥ from partner:

♠ K J 5
♥ 10 4
♦ A J 10 8
♣ K Q 7 6

With a hand of 14 HCPs without support for partner's suit, you could simply start off by bidding a new suit at the two level, 2♣. Because the hand is balanced, some partnerships might prefer to respond 2NT as a forcing bid showing 13–15 points. Other partnerships, using the limited approach, would respond 3NT as an invitational bid showing 13–15 points.

Again, the choice of style is yours. Make sure that partner is on the same wavelength.

A Final Note

Before leaving this chapter, I do have some advice to share. There are some hard-and-fast rules in bridge—each player is dealt thirteen cards, and you do have to follow suit during the play of the cards. Bidding preferences, however, are worked out in your partnership. Don't let your preferences create a wedge between you and your friends. There's no research to prove conclusively, for example, that a raise from 1♥ to 3♥ with 11–12 points is better than using an approach where a raise shows 13–15 points. Choose the style that best suits you.

Summary

When partner opens the bidding 1♥ or 1♠, responder can use the following guidelines based on the strength of the hand:

0–5 points	• Pass.
6–10 points	• Raise partner's major suit to the two level with adequate trump support (three or more cards).
	• Bid a new suit if it can be bid at the one level.
	• Otherwise, bid 1NT.
11–12 points	• Raise partner's major suit to the three level with good trump support.
	• Otherwise, bid a new suit.
13 or more points	• Bid a new suit.

When planning to support partner's major suit, revalue the hand using dummy points, rather than length points:

Dummy Points

Void	5 points
Singleton	3 points
Doubleton	1 point

Exercises

1. What would you respond to an opening bid of 1♥ with each of the following hands?

a) ♠ 10 8 5 2
♥ 5 3
♦ K 8 6 3
♣ J 7 5

b) ♠ 9 4
♥ K 10 3
♦ J 10 7
♣ Q J 8 6 4

c) ♠ Q 10
♥ K J 7 4
♦ 3 2
♣ A 9 8 7 2

d) ♠ A 5
♥ A J 8 2
♦ J 8 7
♣ K J 7 6

e) ♠ 10 9 7
♥ J 10 8 5
♦ 3
♣ K 9 7 6 2

f) ♠ K J 8 7 5
♥ 3
♦ K 9 6 2
♣ 10 8 4

g) ♠ K J 8
♥ 9 3
♦ Q J 7 2
♣ Q 9 6 5

h) ♠ J 3
♥ 5
♦ K 10 4 3 2
♣ K J 7 5 2

i) ♠ 7 4
♥ 8 6
♦ A Q J 8 3
♣ K Q J 5

j) ♠ Q 10 6 2
♥ 7 3
♦ K J 10 7 5
♣ J 5

k) ♠ 2
♥ K 5
♦ A 10 8 6 3
♣ K Q 8 7 3

Answers to Exercises

1a) Pass. With only 4 HCPs there isn't enough strength to respond.

1b) 2♥. This hand has adequate trump support, and falls into the 6–10 point range. Show this by raising partner's suit to the two level.

1c) 3♥. There are 10 HCPs, and you can add 1 dummy point for each doubleton. A jump raise to the three level shows a hand in the 11–12 point range with good support if this is your style. Those playing a jump raise to 3♥ as forcing, would start with 2♣.

1d) 2♣. There are 14 HCPs plus 1 dummy point for the doubleton spade. Partnerships using forcing raises could respond 3♥ with this hand. Those playing limit raises would start with a new suit, 2♣, planning to bid 4♥ at the next opportunity.

1e) 2♥. There are only 4 HCPs, but with good support for partner's suit, you can add 3 dummy points for the singleton diamond. That's enough to raise partner's major suit to the two level.

1f) 1♠. There are 7 HCPs plus 1 point for the five-card suit. That's too much to pass. Without support for partner's major, you can bid a new suit at the one level with 6 or more points.

1g) 1NT. With this hand you can't support partner's suit, and can't bid a new suit at the one level. With only 9 HCPs, there isn't enough strength to bid a new suit at the two level. Instead, respond 1NT, showing a 6–10 point hand.

1h) 1NT. Although the hand is unbalanced, it's similar in nature to the previous example. There are 7 HCPs plus 1 point for each five-card suit. 9 points isn't enough to bid a new suit at the two level. Without support for partner, the only choice is 1NT.

1i) 2♦. There are 13 HCPs plus 1 point for the five-card diamond suit. That's more than enough to bid a new suit at the two level. With a choice of suits, bid the longer.

1j) 1♠. Although you prefer to respond in your longer suit when there's a choice, there isn't enough strength on this hand to bid 2♦. Instead, bid a new suit at the one level, since this can be done with as few as 6 points.

1k) 2♦. This hand has 12 HCPs plus 1 for each of the five-card suits. There's enough strength to bid a new suit at the two level, and with a choice of five-card suits, start with the higher-ranking.

Responding to an Opening Bid of 1♣ or 1♦

"The essentials for playing a good game of bridge are to be truthful, clearheaded, and considerate, prudent but not adverse to taking a risk, and not to cry over spilled milk. And incidentally those are perhaps also the essentials for playing the more important game of life."

— SOMERSET MAUGHAM

My students tell me that responding to an opening bid of 1♣ or 1♦ is harder on the nerves than responding to a major suit opening. I don't think that any part of this game should be hard on the nerves. I'd like to identify some of the areas of discomfort.

The opening bid of one of a minor suit covers a wide range of strength—from about 13 to 21 points—and a variety of distributions—from balanced hands to wildly unbalanced hands. The partnership may feel less relaxed when the bidding starts with one of a minor suit than when it starts with one of a major suit, especially if there's lingering uncertainty about the "short club." An opening bid of 1♥ or 1♠ shows a five-card or longer suit, and responder can feel comfortable with this knowledge. An opening bid of 1♣ or 1♦ could be made with a three-card suit, leaving responder feeling uneasy.

The focus of the bidding conversation, even after a minor suit opening bid, is to find a major suit fit. Opener will often have a four-card major suit when the opening bid is 1♣ or 1♦, since opener would need a five-card suit to mention the major suit initially. Or opener may have support for responder's major suit. There's room to explore after a minor suit opening bid.

As responder, you have the familiar four choices:

- Passing.
- Bidding a suit of your own.
- Supporting partner's suit.
- Bidding notrump.

Responder's bids are either invitational or forcing, since responder doesn't have enough information to make a sign-off bid, placing the contract. There's a difference between responding to a minor suit and responding to a major suit. When the opening bid is 1♣ or 1♦, bidding your own suit takes priority over supporting opener's suit. Let's look in more detail at each of responder's choices.

Passing Time

The guideline for passing when partner opens the bidding in a minor suit is the same as that for major suits:

- With 0–5 points, pass when partner opens the bidding 1♣ or 1♦.

For example, suppose partner opens the bidding 1♣, and this is your hand:

♠ J 8 6 4
♥ 10 5
♦ Q 9 6 4 2
♣ 8 3

Pass. There are only 3 HCPs plus 1 for the five-card suit. The partnership belongs in partscore, even if partner has a strong hand. There may be a better partscore, but it's risky to bid. A new suit by responder is forcing, and opener must bid again. You'll end up in an even higher contract.

There are partners who say, "Don't pass my 1♣ bid. Keep things going with 1♦, even if you have nothing." In standard bidding, however, 1♣ is not a forcing opening bid, and you should feel free to pass when you have less than 6 points. There's no reason to believe that 1♣ isn't the best contract. Partner may have six or seven clubs. If you say something, partner's next bid might be 3♣, or more, and you could end up going from the frying pan into the fire. Time to go quietly.

Searching for a Fit

With more than 5 points, keep the bidding going. There may be enough combined strength for game, even if responder has only 6 points because opener may have started with 20 or 21 points.

When partner opens the bidding at the one level in a minor suit, the search is on for a major suit fit. Suppose partner opens the bidding 1♦, and this is your hand:

♠ A 9 8 7
♥ 4
♦ K Q 8 7 6
♣ Q 8 3

The partnership has at least an eight-card fit in diamonds but remember, showing support for partner's diamonds—a minor suit—

isn't the priority. Respond 1♠. A new suit by responder is forcing. If opener doesn't like spades, responder can always show the diamond support later.

Opener needs a five-card suit to start the bidding in a major suit; responder is under no such restrictions. Responder doesn't need any strength in the suit in order to mention it.

For example, consider this hand after partner opens the bidding 1♣:

> ♠ A 8 3
> ♥ 8 6 5 2
> ♦ J 7
> ♣ K 10 6 3

Respond 1♥, even though there are only four small cards in the suit. You won't be left to play with hearts as the trump suit unless partner has support for the suit.

Familiar Choices

With a choice of suits, bid the longer suit. With two five-card or six-card suits, start with the higher-ranking. For example, consider your response with these hands after partner bids 1♦:

> ♠ Q 10 8 6 5
> ♥ A K 6 2
> ♦ 5 3
> ♣ J 4

With a choice between bidding the five-card spade suit or the four-card heart suit, respond 1♠, the longer suit. If you get an opportunity to bid hearts later in the auction, partner will get the message that you likely have more spades than hearts. It Isn't the strength of the suit that's important, it's the length.

> ♠ 2
> ♥ A Q 10 8 4
> ♦ 9 2
> ♣ A K J 7 3

Respond 1♥. With a choice of five-card suits, start with the higher-ranking.

Responding in your longest suit applies only when you have a choice. Consider this hand after partner opens the bidding 1♦:

> ♠ Q 10 8 5
> ♥ 10 4
> ♦ 9 2
> ♣ A J 8 6 3

Although the clubs are longer than the spades, there's not enough strength to respond 2♣. Responder should have 11 or more points to bid a new suit at the two level. The best you can do is to bid 1♠, showing the four-card suit. This type of hand, however, is the exception to the rule.

Up the Line

With a choice of four-card suits, responder bids the lower-ranking suit. This is referred to as bidding suits *up the line*. For example, suppose partner opens the bidding 1♦, and this is your hand:

> ♠ A K 9 6
> ♥ Q 10 8 4
> ♦ 7 3
> ♣ J 8 2

With a choice of showing the four-card heart suit or the four-card spade suit, bid the lower-ranking, and respond 1♥.

A new suit by responder is forcing, and opener will bid again. The idea behind bidding four-card suits up the line is that, if opener also has four hearts, the eight-card heart fit will be found. If opener doesn't have support for hearts, but has a four-card spade suit, there's still room at the one level for opener to show the spade suit. Again, the eight-card fit in spades will be found.

Here's another example. This time partner opens the bidding 1♣, and this is your hand:

♠ K J 8 5
♥ 9 3
♦ K 10 8 6
♣ A 7 5

Respond 1♦, bidding the lower-ranking of the two four-card suits. Some partnerships prefer to bypass the diamond suit when they have a four-card major suit to show. Unless you have a special agreement to this effect, I recommend that you show your diamond suit. That way, you'll find all your eight-card fits.

To see how bidding up the line would work after you respond 1♦ with the above hand, let's give opener a variety of hands that would be opened 1♣:

1) ♠ A Q 6 2	2) ♠ Q 9 6 2	3) ♠ 3 2
♥ J 7	♥ A Q 7 5	♥ A 5
♦ Q 4	♦ 7 2	♦ A Q 4 3
♣ K J 10 8 2	♣ K Q 6	♣ Q J 9 3 2

With the first hand, opener doesn't have support for your diamond suit. There's still room at the one level to show the spade suit, and opener can bid 1♠ at the next opportunity.

On the second hand, opener has bid 1♣, the better minor suit, with no five-card major, and doesn't have support for diamonds. Opener can continue showing suits up the line by bidding 1♥. When the bidding comes back to you, there's still room to show your spade suit at the one level, and the fit will be found. On this hand, the partnership will have bid all four suits before finding the fit, and will still be at the one level!

On the last hand, the diamond fit will be found right away. This type of hand is the reason you should respond 1♦, rather than 1♠.

The Jump Shift

There are times when responder might want to send a message to opener that the partnership's target should probably be the slam level rather than the game level. Instead of responding in a new suit at the cheapest available level, responder can jump a level of bidding at the same time as shifting to the new suit. This is called a *jump shift*.

The opening bid shows at least 13 points. If responder has 19 or more, the partnership is close to the 33 combined points for a slam contract. For example, suppose the opening bid is 1♣, and you have this hand:

♠ 2
♥ A K Q 10 8 7 4
♦ A 2
♣ K 10 2

There are 16 HCPs plus 3 points for the seven-card suit. Although a response of 1♥ is forcing, responder could send a message about the strength of this hand by jumping to 2♥, one more level than is necessary. This jump shift commits the partnership to the game level, and shows strong interest in a slam contract.

Strong jump shifts have fallen from popularity in recent years. Some partnerships have lowered the requirements to about 16 or 17 points, a hand that has mild slam interest. Other partnerships have dropped the idea altogether, preferring to assign other meanings to jumps in new suits.

Without a firm understanding with partner about the meaning of a jump in a new suit, respond 1♥ with the above hand. It's a forcing bid, and will leave you with lots of room to go exploring for slam after you hear opener's next bid.

Supporting a Minor

Minor suit fits aren't a priority for the partnership. There are times, however, when there's no major suit fit, and the combined hands are unsuitable for a notrump contract. With no four-card or longer major suit to show, responder can consider supporting opener's minor suit.

Trump Support

An opening bid of 1♥ or 1♠ shows a five-card or longer suit, and responder needs only three cards in the suit to consider raising opener's suit.

Let's move across the table and consider some hands that would be opened in a minor suit:

1) ♠ J 5   2) ♠ A K 8   3) ♠ Q J 7 3
   ♥ A 9 3   ♥ K 6 5   ♥ K Q 9 2
   ♦ 7 4   ♦ Q 10 2   ♦ 4 3
   ♣ A Q J 10 6 2   ♣ Q 9 6 3   ♣ A Q 5

Each of these hands would be opened 1♣. The first hand contains a long club suit, and will not require much support from responder to make a good trump suit. On the second hand, opener has a balanced hand too weak to bid 1NT, and clubs is the longest suit. Responder will need at least four-card support to make clubs a viable trump suit. Even if there's an eight-card or longer club fit, the best contract may still be in notrump. On the last hand, opener has bid a three-card suit because the hand is too weak for 1NT, and there's no five-card major suit. Responder will need at least five clubs before the partnership should consider playing the contract with clubs as the trump suit.

Since opener could have as few as three cards for an opening bid of 1♣ or 1♦, responder should have five or more cards to support opener's minor suit. This applies only in response to the opening bid. If opener shows a long minor suit during the auction by bidding the suit more than once, responder can support with fewer cards.

Revaluation

Dummy points can be used when planning to support partner's major suit, since the contract will end up being played with the major suit as trump. Since you rarely end up playing game in a minor suit—preferring to play in 3NT whenever possible—valuing short suits is not always a good idea. Consider this hand, for example:

                    ♠ 5
                    ♥ K 10 6
                    ♦ A J 8 6 5
                    ♣ K 10 7 4

Initially, you would value this as 11 HCPs plus 1 for the five-card diamond suit. Suppose partner opens the bidding 1♦. With no four-card major to show, and with five-card support for partner's minor, you're planning to show your diamond support. Since you intend to raise diamonds, you might use dummy points rather than length points for valuing the distribution. That would make the hand worth 14 points—11 HCPs plus 3 for the singleton spade. Since opener has 13 or more points, it would appear that the partnership has more than 26 combined points and should reach a game contract.

When your fit is in a minor suit, however, the most likely game contract is 3NT, not 5♦. In a notrump contract, the singleton spade will be a liability rather than an asset, so the hand is probably worth only the original 12 points. If you do end up playing with diamonds as trump, a contract of 5♦ usually requires about 28 or 29 combined points. So, in either case, the value of your hand is not enough to commit the partnership to the game level. You'll need opener to have a little extra.

My recommendation is that you don't use dummy points when valuing the hand in support of opener's minor suit until you're certain the contract is going to played with the minor suit as trump. For example, if partner shows a strong hand and you're considering bidding a diamond slam with the above hand, then the value of the singleton spade should be taken into account.

Hitting the Target

Having decided to support partner's minor suit, you now need to communicate the strength of your hand at the same time. There are different methods that can be used. In this book, the style of limit raises is used:

0–5 points	Pass.
6–10 points	Raise to the two level.
11–12 points	Raise to the three level.
13 or more points	Bid a new suit (planning to get to game).

Let's try some hands after partner opens the bidding 1♦.

♠ 8 5
♥ J 5
♦ K J 8 6 2
♣ Q 10 7 4

Respond 2♦. There are 7 HCPs plus 1 point for the five-card suit, putting the hand in the 6–10 point range. There's no four-card or longer major suit to show, and there isn't enough strength to bid a new suit at the two level. Show the diamond support and the strength of the hand by raising to the two level.

♠ 6
♥ Q 9 4
♦ A J 9 8 6 2
♣ K 8 4

Respond 3♦. There are 10 HCPs plus 2 points for the six-card diamond suit, putting the hand in the 11–12 point range. You shouldn't use dummy points to value the single-ton spade because the contract may well end up in notrump, even though you have an unbalanced hand. Assuming your partnership plays limit raises, a jump raise to 3♦ describes this hand. It's an invitational bid. Opener can pass with a minimum opening bid or carry on to game—3NT or 5♦—with a little extra.

This hand would be awkward if your partnership were playing forcing raises, where a jump raise is a forcing bid, showing 13 or more points and committing the partnership to the game level. Not being strong enough for a forcing raise, you would need to "manufacture" a new suit, and bid 2♣. You don't intend to play with clubs as trump, but a new suit is forcing. You can show your diamond support at your next opportunity.

♠ 8
♥ K 5
♦ K Q 10 8 6
♣ A Q 7 3 2

Respond 2♣. With 14 HCPs plus 1 point for each of the five-card suits, there will be enough combined strength in the partnership hands for a game contract. With a hand too strong for a limit raise of 3♦, start by bidding a new suit. This is a forcing bid, and after a further bid from opener, you'll be in a good position to choose the appropriate game contract.

♠ 10 9 7 3
♥ 6 4
♦ A K 10 8 5
♣ K 4

Respond 1♠. With 10 HCPs plus 1 for the fifth diamond, and with five-card support for opener's minor suit, this hand seems perfect for a limit raise to 3♦. Before raising opener's minor suit, however, the priority is to look for a major suit fit. Start by showing your four-card spade suit, even though it looks rather feeble. If partner doesn't like spades, you can show your diamond support later. Partner's hand might be something like this:

♠ A K J 6
♥ Q 3
♦ Q J 9 4 2
♣ Q 3

A game contract of 4♠ would be reasonable. A contract of 5♦ wouldn't stand a chance, since the opponents can take the first three tricks.

Responding in Notrump

There's nothing new here. A response in notrump after a minor suit opening is the same as after a major suit opening.

Responding 1NT

A response of 1NT shows a hand in the 6–10 point range that doesn't have a four-card or longer suit to show at the one level, and doesn't have support for opener's suit. For example, suppose the opening bid is 1♦.

♠ K 10 5
♥ K J 5
♦ 10 8 2
♣ Q 10 6 2

Respond 1NT. There are 9 HCPs, not enough to venture into a new suit at the two level. There's no four-card suit that can be bid at the one level, and three cards in diamonds aren't enough to support partner's minor suit. The hand falls nicely into the 1NT category.

♠ 7 4
♥ A 2
♦ 8 4
♣ Q 10 7 6 4 3 2

Respond 1NT. This is the not-so-nice hand that still falls into the 1NT category. There are 6 HCPs plus 3 for the seven-card suit. That's too much to pass—partner might have a very strong hand of about 20 points. On the other hand, you don't have the 11 or more points needed to bid a new suit at the two level. That would be a forcing bid, and the partnership might get much too high with no suitable place to play the hand. With no other suit to bid, and no support for partner's suit, the only choice left is the 1NT bid.

Although the initial response is 1NT, that doesn't end the auction, and you may get an opportunity to show your club suit later. 1NT is an invitational response, and if opener bids again, you might show your club suit, safe in the knowledge that you've already limited the strength of your hand to 6–10 points. Opener can then act accordingly.

The 2NT and 3NT Responses

There are two popular styles when responding in notrump to a minor suit. The first is:

1NT	6–10 points. This is the invitational response discussed above.
2NT	13–15 points. This is a forcing response showing a balanced hand. In most partnerships, responder can't have a four-card major suit to make this response.
3NT	16–18 points. This shows a balanced hand, and isn't forcing. Again, in most partnerships, responder wouldn't have a four-card major suit when choosing this response.

With 11–12 points, and a balanced hand, responder would start by bidding a new suit, intending to make an invitational bid of 2NT at the next opportunity.

The other popular style is to follow the limit raise approach:

1NT   6–10 points. This is the same under either approach.

2NT   11–12 points. This is an invitational response showing a balanced hand without a four-card or longer major suit.

3NT   13–15 points. This shows a balanced hand without a four-card or longer major suit, and isn't forcing.

Using this style, responder would start with a new suit when holding a hand of 16 or more points, planning to show the extra strength later.

Here are some examples after an opening bid of 1♦:

♠ K 10 8
♥ A Q 5
♦ J 8 7 4
♣ K J 6

Using the first approach, this hand could respond 2NT, forcing, showing a balanced hand of 13–15 points. In the limit raise style, responder would bid 3NT with this hand.

♠ A J 4
♥ Q J 7
♦ Q 9 6
♣ J 10 6 3

With 11 HCPs, and a balanced hand, responder would start with a new suit, 2♣, under the first approach, planning to bid notrump at the next opportunity. Using limit raises, you could immediately respond 2NT with this hand, an invitational bid showing 11–12 points.

♠ A Q 9
♥ K 10 3
♦ Q 9 6
♣ A Q J 3

With a balanced hand of 18 points, you could respond 3NT if your partnership uses the first approach—where this response shows a balanced hand with the same strength as an opening 1NT bid. If your partnership style is that a 3NT response would show a hand of only 13–15 points, you would start with a new suit, 2♣, and show the extra strength later.

♠ K Q 5
♥ Q 10 6 2
♦ K 8 3
♣ A 7 5

Respond 1♥. Although this is a balanced hand, most partnerships would start by showing the four-card major suit before bidding notrump, in case the partnership has an eight-card major suit fit.

Agree with your partner on the style of notrump responses you would like to use. If you have no agreement, you can always avoid responding 2NT or 3NT. Start by responding in a new suit, and show the balanced hand at the next opportunity. In this book, the limit raise approach will be used.

Summary

When partner opens the bidding 1♣ or 1♦, responder can use the following guidelines based on the strength of the hand:

0–5 points	• Pass.
6–10 points	• Bid a new suit if it can be bid at the one level.
	• Raise partner's minor suit to the two level with five-card or longer support.
	• Otherwise, bid 1NT.
11–12 points	• Bid a new suit.
	• Raise partner's minor suit to the three level with five-card or longer support.
	• Bid 2NT (if the partnership uses limit raises).
13 or more points	• Bid a new suit.
	• Bid 3NT (if the partnership uses the limit raise approach) or 2NT (if the partnership uses the forcing approach).

Exercises

1. What would you respond to 1♣ with each of the following hands?

a) ♠ 5 4 3
♥ K 9 7 3
♦ J 8 4 2
♣ 6 4

b) ♠ K 10 9 6 4
♥ K J 5 2
♦ A 5
♣ Q 10

c) ♠ Q 9 6 3
♥ K 10 7 5
♦ J 8 5
♣ A 7

d) ♠ A J 8 6 2
♥ K Q 8 6 3
♦ 7
♣ J 6

e) ♠ 9 7
♥ 10 8 5
♦ A 7 3
♣ K 9 7 6 2

f) ♠ K 8 6 5
♥ 9 2
♦ 6 5
♣ K J 10 8 3

2. What would you respond to 1♦ with each of the following hands?

a) ♠ J 3
♥ K 9 4
♦ J 6 5
♣ Q 10 8 6 2

b) ♠ A 5
♥ 10 8
♦ K J 8 6 2
♣ K 10 6 5

c) ♠ 6 3
♥ A Q 7 5
♦ 10 3
♣ A K J 8 3

d) ♠ K 10 5
♥ A J 10
♦ K 8 3 2
♣ Q 6 2

e) ♠ 6
♥ A 10
♦ K Q 9 7 3
♣ A 10 8 6 3

f) ♠ 3
♥ A K J 10 8 6
♦ K Q 4
♣ A Q 5

Answers to Exercises

1a) Pass. With a hand in the 0–5 range, you don't have enough to respond.

1b) 1♠. The first priority is to bid a new suit, looking for a fit. With a choice of suits, bid the longer. A new suit by responder is forcing, so there's no fear of missing a game contract with your 13 HCPs and 1 point for the five-card spade suit. After opener's next bid you'll be better positioned to decide on a suitable game contract.

1c) 1♥. With a choice between four-card suits to show at the one level, start with the lower-ranking, hearts. This is bidding the four-card suits up the line.

1d) 1♠. With a choice between two five-card suits, bid the higher-ranking, spades. If opener doesn't like spades, you can show the heart suit at your next opportunity.

1e) 2♣. With five-card support for opener's minor suit, and no other suit to show at the one level, raise opener's suit. With 7 HCPs plus 1 for the fifth club, the hand falls into the 6–10 point range, which is shown by a raise to the two level.

1f) 1♠. Although this hand has support for opener's minor suit, the first priority is to search for a major suit fit. If there's no partnership fit in spades, you can return to clubs later.

2a) 1NT. With only 7 HCPs plus 1 for the five-card suit, there's not enough strength to bid a new suit at the two level. With no suit to bid at the one level, and without support for opener's minor suit, the hand drops into the 1NT category.

2b) 3♦. There are 11 HCPs plus 1 for the five-card diamond suit. If the partnership uses the limit raise approach, a response of 3♦ shows the support for opener's suit and an invitational hand in the 11–12 point range. If the partnership uses forcing raises, responder would start off by bidding 2♣, a new suit, intending to show the diamond support on the next round of bidding.

2c) 2♣. With 14 HCPs plus 1 for the five-card club suit, there's enough strength to bid a new suit at the two level. With a choice of suits, bid the longer suit. The hand is strong enough to show the heart suit later in the auction, and opener will then know that you have more clubs than hearts.

2d) **3NT** (2NT). With a balanced hand and 13 HCPs the choice of response depends on the partnership style. Playing limit raises, this hand would respond 3NT showing 13–15 points, a balanced hand and no four-card major suit. Playing forcing raises, a response of 2NT would show this hand.

2e) **2♣** (3♦). With 13 HCPs plus 2 for the two five-card suits, this hand is strong enough to commit the partnership to a game contract. Playing a limit raise approach, the hand is too strong to respond 2♦. Start with a new suit, 2♣, intending to bid diamonds later. If the partnership style is forcing raises, then a response of 3♦ is a forcing bid and can be used to tell partner right away about the diamond support and the strength of the hand.

2f) **1♥** (2♥). A response of 1♥ is a forcing bid, and responder can start with this, planning to show the extra strength after hearing opener's next bid. Alternatively, responder can show the great strength immediately by making a jump shift response of 2♥, telling opener that the partnership should be targeting the slam level, rather than the game level.

Part 4

THE PLOT
THICKENS—
ALL ABOUT REBIDS

Opener's Rebids After an Opening Notrump Bid

"I would have written you a shorter letter, but I didn't have the time."

This is a short chapter because the notrump opening bid just about says it all. It describes opener's distribution as being balanced and places opener's strength within a narrow range of points. This puts responder in a good position to act as captain, and make a decision about the contract. Responder sends a suitable sign-off message, and opener has nothing further to do.

There are times when responder needs more information from opener. Responder makes a bid that carries an invitational or forcing message. When it comes time for opener to make a second bid, *opener's rebid*, a suitable reply must be given to responder's message.

Passing Time

If responder makes a sign-off bid, opener is expected to pass. Responder has taken the information provided by the original notrump opening bid and decided that it's sufficient to settle on a contract for the partnership. For example, suppose you open the bidding 1NT with this hand:

> ♠ K J 8 5
> ♥ 3 2
> ♦ A Q 8 4
> ♣ A Q 10

If partner responds 2♥, you would pass when the bidding comes back to you. You may not like partner's choice of 2♥ as the contract for your side, but partner's bid carries a sign-off message. Partner knows a lot about your hand from the opening 1NT bid. You know very little about partner's hand. You shouldn't try to override the captain's choice by bidding 2NT. For example, partner's hand might be something like this:

> ♠ 4
> ♥ Q 10 9 8 7 5 4
> ♦ 9 3
> ♣ J 8 2

2♥ is the best partscore for your side. Anything you do to try to "improve" the contract is unlikely to work.

The same principle applies if your opening bid is 2NT or 3NT. For example, suppose you open the bidding 2NT with this hand:

> ♠ A Q J
> ♥ K Q J
> ♦ K Q 4
> ♣ A J 8 3

If partner responds 4♠, you should pass. You have a great hand, with good support for partner's spades, but you showed your strength and distribution when you opened 2NT. Nothing has changed because of partner's 4♠ response. Just put your dummy down with a smile!

Help Wanted

Partner may require your help in deciding on the contract. If partner's bid carries a forcing message, you can't pass when it comes time to make your rebid. For example, suppose you open the bidding 1NT with this hand:

♠ K J 5
♥ A Q
♦ A 9 6 2
♣ Q J 8 4

If partner were to respond 3♥, that would be a forcing bid asking you to choose between 3NT and 4♥. Responder is showing the values for a game contract and only a five-card heart suit. Responder wants your help in deciding whether or not the partnership has an eight-card heart fit. With only a doubleton heart, choose 3NT rather than 4♥.

If partner were to respond 3♠, you would rebid 4♠, since you have three-card support for partner's suit. Partner is interested in how many spades you have, not how many points you have in the suit.

Sharing Time

Responder's other message is an invitational one. Responder needs your help to decide if the partnership has enough combined strength for a game or a slam. Suppose you open 1NT with this hand:

♠ Q 10 5
♥ A J 10
♦ K Q 8 6 3
♣ A J

A bid of 2NT by responder is invitational. Pass with the lower end of your promised range. Carry on to game if your strength lies in the upper portion of the range. With 17 HCPs plus 1 for the five-card diamond suit, you're at the top end of the 1NT range, and would accept partner's invitation by bidding 3NT. If your ♦Q were the ♦2, you would be at the bottom of the range, and would decline the invitation by passing.

Suppose you opened 1NT with this hand, and your partner raised to 4NT:

♠ Q 9 8 4
♥ K Q 7 6
♦ A 7
♣ K Q 2

The raise to 4NT is an invitational bid, asking you to choose between 4NT and 6NT, a slam contract. With only 16 HCPs, decline the invitation by passing. If you held a little more, you could carry on to slam by bidding 6NT.

Summary

When it comes time to make a rebid after opening with a notrump bid, listen to the message being sent by responder

- If responder has made a sign-off bid, pass.
- If responder has made a forcing bid, make a rebid that further describes your hand.
- If responder has made an invitational bid, pass with the minimum end of your notrump range, otherwise accept the invitation.

Exercises

1. You open the bidding 1NT with this hand:

♠ Q 4
♥ A 10 8 3
♦ K Q 10
♣ A K 9 2

What would you rebid:

a) If responder bid 2♦?
b) If responder bid 2♠?
c) If responder bid 2NT?
d) If responder bid 3♥?
e) If responder bid 3♠?
f) If responder bid 3NT?
g) If responder bid 4♠?
h) If responder bid 4NT?
i) If responder bid 6NT?

Answers to Exercises

a) **Pass**. Responder's bid is a sign-off.

b) **Pass**. Responder's bid is a sign-off.

c) **3NT**. Responder's bid is an invitation, and you're at the upper end of the notrump range.

d) **4♥**. Responder's bid is forcing, asking you to choose between 3NT and 4♥. With four-card support for responder's suit, choose game in the suit.

e) **3NT**. Responder's bid is forcing, asking you to choose between 3NT and 4♠. With only a doubleton spade, choose 3NT.

f) **Pass**. Responder's bid is a sign-off bid.

g) **Pass**. Responder's bid is a sign-off bid.

h) **6NT**. Responder's bid is an invitation asking you to decide between stopping in 4NT and carrying on to 6NT. With the top of your notrump range, carry on to slam.

i) **Pass**. Responder's bid is a sign-off bid. Responder has decided that there's enough combined strength to play in a small slam contract.

Opener's Rebids After One-of-a-Suit Openings

"When your bidding is more work than play, simplify your bidding system; what you leave out could be more important than what you include!"

This is one of my favorite topics or, should I say, it used to be. Whenever I was teaching a class and it came time for the lesson on rebids by opener, I illustrated the concept of classifying opener's strength by referring to *Goldilocks and the Three Bears*. A minimum, Baby Bear, hand was one with 13–16 points; a medium, Mama Bear, hand contained 17–18 points; a maximum, Papa Bear, hand was 19–21 points. I even had pictures of the bears, looking something like this:

Minimum Hand	Medium Hand	Maximum Hand
13 14 15 16	17 18	19 20 21

One day, while traveling on the subway, I overheard two people discussing bridge lessons. One of them mentioned my name, praising my use of the three-bear analogy. I couldn't see the face of the other student but will never forget the intonation in the voice as the reaction came: "I could never respect a teacher who has to revert to fairy tales to get the point across." And so, that evening, I took the pictures down to the basement where they gathered dust for a while before being discarded. If you do find the parallel helpful, don't tell anyone; if you find it offensive, pretend I didn't mention the three bears at all.

The Big Picture

Both partners are trying to describe their strength and distribution as quickly as possible during the bidding process. As soon as one player can put some specific limits on the strength and the shape of the hand, the other player can take on the role of captain, and place the contract. A 1NT opening limits the strength of the hand within a three-point range, and, at the same time, describes a balanced distribution. After that, responder is often able to make a sign-off bid, and put the contract at the partscore, game, or slam level. When this is the case, opener is expected to pass.

When you start the bidding with one-of-a-suit, your hand falls into a wide range of strength between 13 and 21 points. You can also have a variety of distributions, from very balanced hands to wildly unbalanced hands. Responder is not in a position to place the contract. Instead, responder makes an invitational or forcing response, waiting for a further description of your hand.

When making a rebid as opener, your role is to further clarify the range of your strength and the distribution of your hand. You try to make a rebid that puts the strength of your hand into one of three categories:

13–16 points	a minimum-strength one-level opening bid
17–18 points	a medium-strength one-level opening bid
19–21 points	a maximum-strength one-level opening bid

At the same time, you want to further describe your distribution. If responder has made a forcing bid by bidding a new suit, you have to bid again and have a number of choices:

- Supporting responder's suit.
- Bidding a new suit at the one level.
- Bidding notrump.
- Bidding a new suit at the two level or higher.
- Rebidding your own suit.

If responder has made an invitational bid, such as raising your suit, then you can pass or bid on. Let's look at each situation in turn.

Supporting Responder's Suit

The partnership is searching for a trump fit. If partner doesn't support your suit, the first priority on your rebid is to try to support partner's suit.

An opening bid of 1♥ or 1♠ shows a five-card suit, and responder can raise with only three-card support. A response in a new suit, however, can be made on any four-card suit, so opener should usually have four cards in the suit to consider raising.

If you're planning to raise partner's suit, you can revalue your hand using dummy points—5 for a void, 3 for a singleton, 1 for a doubleton—rather than length points. This works in the same way as when responder is raising your suit.

Let's look at some examples. Suppose you open the bidding 1♦ with the following hand, and partner responds 1♠:

♠ K 9 8 3
♥ A 5
♦ Q J 8 7
♣ K 10 2

Partner didn't support your diamond suit, but has shown at least a four-card spade suit. You also have four spades; there's an eight-card major suit fit. Let partner know. What do you want to say about the strength of your hand? With only 13 HCPs, it's a minimum-strength hand. You're planning to support partner's suit, so you can count 1 dummy point for the doubleton heart, but you're still in the minimum range. Since partner's 1♠ bid is forcing, you can't pass, but with a minimum-strength hand, you don't want to get too high. Rebid 2♠. That will tell partner that you like spades, and since you've raised only to the next available level, partner will get the message that you have the minimum range for an opening bid, about 13–16 points. Partner can take it from there.

Suppose the auction goes the same way, but this is your hand:

♠ A J 8 3
♥ 4
♦ K Q 10 9 4
♣ A 8 2

You start by valuing the hand as 15 points—14 HCPs plus 1 point for the five-card diamond suit—and open the bidding 1♦. When partner responds 1♠, you can revalue the hand using dummy points. Because of the spade support, the hand is now worth 17 points—14 HCPs plus 3 for the singleton heart. That puts it in the medium-strength category. You can get the message across to partner about the support and the strength by jumping to 3♠, rather than raising to 2♠. That sounds "mediumish." 2♠ is too small; 4♠ is too large; 3♠ is just right!

Try this hand, with the auction also starting with 1♦ by you and 1♠ by partner:

♠ A Q 8 4
♥ Q 9 7
♦ A Q J 6 5 2
♣ —

You have 15 HCPs plus 5 dummy points for the club void. Raise partner's 1♠ response all the way to 4♠. After all, partner needs at least 6 points to respond at the one level, and you have 20. The partnership should have the 26 combined points necessary for a game contract.

Continuing up the Line

If you haven't found a fit by the time the bidding comes back to you, there may be room left at the one level to show another suit. This is a continuation of the style of bidding suits up the line. For example, suppose you start the bidding 1♣, partner responds 1♥, and the auction comes back to you with this hand:

♠ Q 10 9 5
♥ Q 6
♦ A 8
♣ A Q 7 3 2

Partner didn't support your clubs, and you don't have support for partner's hearts. There's still room left at the one level to show your spade suit. Rebid 1♠. This will allow the partnership to find its spade fit if responder's hand looks something like this:

♠ K J 6 2
♥ J 10 8 5
♦ J 5 2
♣ 8 4

By responding 1♥, partner was following the guideline of bidding four-card suits up the line—lower-ranking first. The bidding conversation works well by exchanging all the necessary information to find a fit while remaining at the one level.

Even with a medium-strength hand of 17–18 points, opener still bids a new suit at the one level, rather than jumping to the two level to show the extra strength. For example, suppose you open the bidding 1♦ with this hand, and partner responds 1♥:

> ♠ A Q 8 3
> ♥ 4
> ♦ K Q J 9 6 2
> ♣ K 8

There are 15 HCPs plus 2 for the six-card suit, putting this hand in the medium-strength category. Since the partnership is still searching for a fit, it would take up a lot of bidding room if you were to jump to 2♠ with this sort of hand. The partnership might end up too high. Instead, rebid 1♠, planning to show the extra strength after you've found a fit with partner.

With a maximum-strength hand, however, you can jump one level to show the great strength. This is a *jump shift* by opener to show 19 or more points, similar to a jump shift by responder. For example:

> ♠ A K J 3
> ♥ K 6
> ♦ A Q J 10 8 7
> ♣ 2

You start the bidding with 1♦, and responder bids 1♥. With 18 HCPs plus 2 points for the six-card suit, you're strong enough to jump shift to 2♠, rather than bidding 1♠.

A jump shift by opener commits the partnership to the game level, since opener is showing about 20 points and responder must have at least 6 points to bid at the one level.

Showing Balance

If you can't find a fit at the one level, opener's next option is to show a balanced hand by rebidding in notrump. Since a balanced hand of 16–18 points would be opened 1NT, there are only two types of balanced hands opener can have: hands of 13–15 points that are too weak to open 1NT; hands of 19–21 points that are too strong to open 1NT. Opener shows the 13–15 point range by bidding notrump at the cheapest available level. The strong hands are shown by jumping in notrump.

For example, suppose you start the bidding 1♦ with this hand, and partner responds 1♥:

> ♠ K J 6
> ♥ J 5
> ♦ A J 8 2
> ♣ K 10 8 3

You can't support partner's suit and don't have another suit that can be shown at the one level. You do have a four-card club suit, but you would have to go to the two level to show it. Instead, you can describe the balanced nature of your hand by rebidding 1NT. Since you didn't open the bidding 1NT, responder will get the message that you have a balanced hand too weak to open 1NT. That's a hand in the 13–15 point range.

Suppose the auction goes the same way, and this is your hand:

> ♠ A Q 5
> ♥ Q 6
> ♦ K J 10 8 7
> ♣ A Q 4

This time you have 19 points—18 HCPs plus 1 point for the fifth diamond. The hand is balanced, but is too strong to open 1NT, so start with your longest suit, 1♦. When it comes to your rebid, you can't support partner's heart suit and don't have a four-card spade suit to show. Instead, you can jump to 2NT to describe both your shape and strength. Responder will decide on the best contract for the partnership.

New Suits at the Two Level or Higher

Without a balanced hand, you can't rebid in notrump. If you can't support partner's suit, and there's no room left to show your suit at the one level, your choice is between showing a new suit or rebidding your original suit. Usually, you show the second suit. For example:

♠ 3
♥ A Q 8 6 2
♦ 7 5
♣ A K 10 6 2

You start the bidding with the higher-ranking of your five-card suits, 1♥, and partner responds 1♠. Partner hasn't supported your suit, and you don't have support for partner's suit. There's no room left to show another suit at the one level, and you can't rebid notrump because your hand isn't balanced. Instead, show your second suit by bidding 2♣. Partner will now know that you have at least five hearts and at least four clubs. This will help partner decide where the partnership belongs.

I'd like to have avoided the statement that you usually show your second suit. You can always show a second suit at the two level that's lower-ranking than your original suit, as in the above example—clubs are lower-ranking than diamonds. This is because, even with a minimum-strength hand of about 6–10 points, responder will always be able to choose between your suits at the two level. In the above example, if responder prefers clubs to hearts as the trump suit, and has a weak hand, responder can pass, leaving the partnership to play a partscore contract of 2♣. Preferring hearts to clubs, responder can go back to 2♥, and the partnership can again play in a partscore at the two level.

Things are a little more awkward when opener's second suit is higher-ranking than the original suit. For example, suppose you open the bidding 1♦ with this hand, and partner responds 1♠:

♠ 4
♥ K J 8 2
♦ A Q J 8 6 3
♣ Q 8

Partner didn't support your suit, you don't have support for partner's suit, and you don't have a balanced hand. To show your second suit, hearts, you would have to bid 2♥ because there's no room left to show a new suit at the one level. That will be fine if responder prefers hearts to diamonds. It won't be such a good idea if responder prefers diamonds. Responder will have to go to the three level and bid 3♦ to play with that suit as trump. This may get the partnership too high when responder has a minimum hand of about 6 points, and the partnership ends up playing at the three level. If responder doesn't like either of your suits, things might get worse. You'll already be at the two level, still searching for a place to play.

On such hands, it's better to rebid your first suit, 2♦, to avoid getting the partnership too high. The guideline is this:

- With a minimum-strength hand, bid a new suit at the two level only if it's lower-ranking than your original suit.

You have to use this guideline only when you have a minimum-strength hand. With a medium-strength or maximum-strength hand, there are no such constraints. For example, suppose you open 1♣ with this hand, and partner responds 1♠:

♠ Q 5
♥ A Q J 8
♦ 9 4
♣ A K J 6 2

There are 17 HCPs plus 1 point for the five-card suit, putting this hand in the medium category. With the extra strength, you can afford to show your second suit at the two level by bidding 2♥, even though it's higher-ranking than your original suit. If responder has a minimum hand without support for hearts, and has to go back to 3♣, your extra strength should help to make sure that the partnership is not too high.

Bidding a new suit at the two level that's higher-ranking than your original suit is called a *reverse*, since the more "natural" way to show a two-suited hand is by starting with the higher-ranking suit, and then bidding the lower-ranking suit. A reverse shows at least a medium-strength hand.

With a maximum-strength hand, you can show the extra strength by jumping in your second suit. This is the jump shift we've encountered before. For example:

♠ 4
♥ A 3
♦ A K J 5 2
♣ A K 10 7 4

You open the bidding 1♦, and partner responds 1♥. Although you could show your second suit by bidding 2♣, that would sound like a minimum-strength hand. With a hand worth 21 points—19 HCPs plus 1 for each five-card suit—you can show the extra strength by jumping to 3♣. This is done only with a maximum-strength hand, since the jump commits the partnership to the game level.

The Same Old Tune

If you have an unbalanced hand, and no second suit that can be shown, you simply rebid your original suit. For example:

♠ 4 3
♥ A Q J 8 6 2
♦ 10 5
♣ A J 4

You open the bidding 1♥, and partner responds 1♠. You can't support partner's suit, and your hand is unbalanced, so you can't rebid in notrump. With no second suit to show, rebid 2♥. You have a minimum-strength hand, so you make a minimum-sounding rebid by bidding your original suit again at the cheapest available level.

Suppose the auction goes the same way, and you have a little more strength:

♠ 4 3
♥ A K J 10 8 6
♦ 10 5
♣ A K 3

Rebid 3♥. The hand is worth 17 points—15 HCPs plus 2 points for the six-card heart suit. Show this hand by jumping a level, rather than rebidding your suit at the cheapest level. This is only an invitational bid, but it shows a little extra for your opening bid.

Then there's the maximum-strength hand:

♠ 3
♥ A K Q 10 8 7 3
♦ J 5
♣ A K 3

With 17 HCPs plus 3 points for the seven-card suit, you can describe this hand by rebidding 4♥. Since you have 20 points, and responder has at least 6 points, there should be enough combined strength for a game contract, even when responder has no support for your suit.

Responder Limits the Hand— By Making a Raise

If responder makes a limit—invitational—raise of your suit, you don't have to bid. Follow this basic principle: the more you have, the more you bid. For example, suppose the bidding starts this way:

OPENER	RESPONDER
1♥	2♥
?	

Responder has shown support for your suit, and about 6–10 points. The raise to 2♥ is an invitational bid. Responder can't decide whether the partnership belongs in partscore or game because responder doesn't know the exact strength of your hand. Suppose you have a minimum-strength hand:

♠ J 8 4
♥ K 10 9 7 5
♦ A 10 4
♣ K Q

There are 13 HCPs plus 1 for the five-card suit. Since responder has made a bid limited to at most 10 points, the partnership belongs in partscore. You should pass. You don't have to bid because the partnership has already found the best contract.

Suppose you hold a medium-strength hand:

♠ J 4
♥ K Q J 7 6 2
♦ Q 8 3
♣ A Q

There are 15 HCPs plus 2 points for the six-card suit. Partner's raise shows 6–10 points. If partner is at the bottom end of the range, 6–8 points, there won't be enough combined strength for game. If partner is at the top end of the range, 9–10 points, there should be enough for game. You have too much to pass, but too little to go all the way to game by yourself. Instead, rebid 3♥, the medium-sounding bid.

The same concept applies to the maximum-strength hand:

♠ 10 4
♥ A K J 8 7 3
♦ K 8 2
♣ A K

There are 18 HCPs plus 2 points for the six-card suit. You can make the maximum-sounding bid by jumping all the way to game, 4♥. The more you have, the more you bid.

Responder Limits the Hand— By Bidding Notrump

Opener can use all the same principles if responder makes a limited, invitational, response by bidding notrump rather than raising opener's suit. For example, suppose the auction starts this way:

OPENER	RESPONDER
1♦	1NT
?	

♠ J 5
♥ K 10 8
♦ A Q 7 5 2
♣ Q J 6

Pass. You have 13 HCPs plus 1 point for the five-card suit. Responder's bid shows a limited hand of about 6–10 points. The most the partnership could hold is 24 points (14 + 10). There could be as few as 20 combined points (14 + 6), so the partnership belongs in a partscore. Since you have a balanced hand, the best partscore appears to be right where you are, 1NT.

♠ A J 8 7
♥ K Q 9 4
♦ A 6 3
♣ 7 4

Pass. Holding only 14 HCPs, and with responder limited to 10 points at most, the partnership belongs in partscore. There's no reason to mention the hearts or spades. Responder would have bid 1♥ or 1♠ with a four-card or longer suit, rather than bidding 1NT. The search is over. You're in the best contract.

♠ 6
♥ Q 9 5
♦ K J 10 8 7 5 2
♣ A 4

2♦. Since you have a minimum hand, the partnership belongs in partscore. With such an unbalanced hand, a partscore of 2♦ would be better than 1NT.

♠ Q 4
♥ K J 4
♦ A K J 10 8 3 2
♣ 7

3♦. This is a medium-sized hand with 14 HCPs plus 3 points for the seven-card suit. Jump to 3♦ to show the extra strength. Responder can pass with the bottom end of the range, 6–8 points, and carry on to game with the top of the range, 9–10 points.

♠ K J
♥ K Q 8 3
♦ A K 8 2
♣ A 10 5

3NT. With a maximum-strength hand of 20 HCPs, take partner right to the game level. There's no need to show the heart suit. Partner would respond 1♥, rather than 1NT, holding a four-card or longer heart suit.

Summary

After opening the bidding, listen to responder's message before making your rebid. If responder has made an invitational bid, such as a raise of your suit or a response of 1NT, you don't have to bid again. If responder has made a forcing bid, such as the bid of a new suit, you must bid again.

Before making your rebid, classify the strength of your hand:

- Minimum: 13–16 points.
- Medium: 17–18 points.
- Maximum: 19–21 points.

Then choose the rebid that best describes both the strength and distribution of your hand. If responder has made a forcing bid, you have a number of choices:

- Supporting responder's suit.
- Bidding a new suit at the one level.
- Bidding notrump.
- Bidding a new suit at the two level or higher.
- Rebidding your own suit.

You can generally follow the guideline that the more you have, the more you bid.

Exercises

1. What would you rebid with each of the following hands after the auction starts:

OPENER	RESPONDER
1♣	1♥
?	

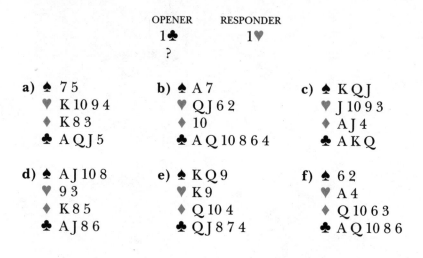

a) ♠ 7 5
   ♥ K 10 9 4
   ♦ K 8 3
   ♣ A Q J 5

b) ♠ A 7
   ♥ Q J 6 2
   ♦ 10
   ♣ A Q 10 8 6 4

c) ♠ K Q J
   ♥ J 10 9 3
   ♦ A J 4
   ♣ A K Q

d) ♠ A J 10 8
   ♥ 9 3
   ♦ K 8 5
   ♣ A J 8 6

e) ♠ K Q 9
   ♥ K 9
   ♦ Q 10 4
   ♣ Q J 8 7 4

f) ♠ 6 2
   ♥ A 4
   ♦ Q 10 6 3
   ♣ A Q 10 8 6

2. What would you rebid with each of the following hands after the auction starts:

OPENER	RESPONDER
1♥	1♠
?	

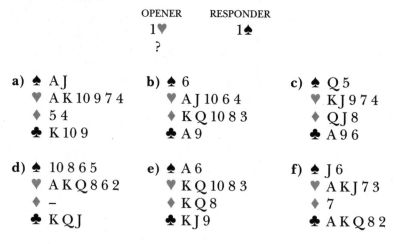

a) ♠ A J
   ♥ A K 10 9 7 4
   ♦ 5 4
   ♣ K 10 9

b) ♠ 6
   ♥ A J 10 6 4
   ♦ K Q 10 8 3
   ♣ A 9

c) ♠ Q 5
   ♥ K J 9 7 4
   ♦ Q J 8
   ♣ A 9 6

d) ♠ 10 8 6 5
   ♥ A K Q 8 6 2
   ♦ –
   ♣ K Q J

e) ♠ A 6
   ♥ K Q 10 8 3
   ♦ K Q 8
   ♣ K J 9

f) ♠ J 6
   ♥ A K J 7 3
   ♦ 7
   ♣ A K Q 8 2

3. What would you rebid with each of the following hands after the auction starts:

OPENER	RESPONDER
1♠	2♠
?	

a) ♠ A Q 8 6 3
  ♥ 7 6
  ♦ A Q 9 4
  ♣ 9 7

b) ♠ K Q 10 8 7
  ♥ K Q 7
  ♦ J
  ♣ A Q J 5

c) ♠ Q 10 9 7 6 5
  ♥ A 8 2
  ♦ A K
  ♣ Q 7

Answers to Exercises

1a) **2♥**. There are 13 HCPs, and with four-card support for responder's suit, you can add 1 point for the doubleton spade. With a minimum hand, make a minimum raise to the next level.

1b) **3♥**. There are 13 HCPs plus 3 dummy points for the singleton diamond and 1 dummy point for the doubleton spade. That puts the hand in the medium-strength category. Jump to 3♥ to show both the support and the strength.

1c) **4♥**. 21 HCPs makes this a maximum-strength hand. With four-card support for partner's suit, raise all the way to the game level.

1d) **1♠**. Without support for responder's suit, there's still room to show another suit at the one level. If responder has four spades, the fit will be found.

1e) **1NT**. You can't support partner's suit and don't have another suit to show at the one level. With a minimum balanced hand of 14 points—13 HCPs plus 1 for the fifth club—finish describing your hand to partner by rebidding notrump at the cheapest available level.

1f) **2♣**. This is an awkward hand. You have a second suit to show but could do so only by bidding it at the two level. With a minimum-strength hand, you shouldn't bid a new suit at the two level that's higher-ranking than your original suit. That would be a reverse and would show extra strength. Instead, rebid your original suit.

2a) **3♥**. This hand is worth 17 points—15 HCPs plus 2 points for the six-card suit. That puts it in the medium-strength category. With an unbalanced hand, and no second suit to show, rebid your suit with a jump to show the extra strength.

2b) **2♦**. With a minimum-strength hand, a second suit can be shown at the two level if it's lower-ranking than your original suit.

2c) **1NT**. You have a minimum balanced hand of 14 points—13 HCPs plus 1 for the five-card heart suit. By rebidding 1NT you show a balanced hand too weak to open the bidding 1NT originally.

2d) **4♠.** Although you have a fine heart suit, you also have support for partner's spade suit, and that takes priority. You have 15 HCPs, and can count 5 dummy points for the diamond void when raising partner's suit. That makes it a maximum-strength hand. Take partner right to the game level.

2e) **2NT.** With 18 HCPs plus 1 for the five-card suit, your hand is too strong to open the bidding 1NT. You describe this hand by opening your long suit and then jumping in notrump to show a maximum-strength balanced hand.

2f) **3♣.** Although you could show your second suit by bidding 2♣, this hand is in the maximum-strength range—18 HCPs plus 1 point for each of the five-card suits. This can be shown by making a jump shift on your rebid. A jump shift commits the partnership to at least the game level.

3a) **Pass.** Partner's raise is invitational, showing spade support and 6–10 points. With a minimum-strength hand of 12 HCPs plus 1 for the five-card suit, the partnership belongs in partscore.

3b) **4♠.** You have 18 HCPs plus 1 point for the fifth spade. That puts the hand in the maximum-strength category, enough to take the partnership to the game level.

3c) **3♠.** This hand is worth 17 points—15 HCPs plus 2 points for the six-card suit. That's a medium-strength hand, so take a medium action by raising to 3♠. With only 6 or 7 points, responder will pass. With 9 or 10, responder will carry on to game.

Rebids
by Responder

> "Begin at the beginning . . . and go on till you
> come to the end: then stop."
>
> —LEWIS CARROLL,
> Alice's Adventures in Wonderland

During the auction, the partnership has a conversation to decide
the best contract. The conversation is similar to other discussions
when two people are trying to reach a consensus. Even simple agreements, such as what to have for dinner, can at times prove challenging. The longer the dialogue continues, the more challenging it can
become. Does this sound familiar?

"Let's go out for dinner."

"I'd love to. Where would you like to go?"

"Anywhere that you want."

"I'd like to go to Anthony's."

"Sounds fine. Do you want to try that new place that just opened?"

"No I'd like to go to Anthony's, but if you want to go to the new
place..."

"No, I thought you liked to try new places."

By the time it's responder's turn to make a rebid, there has already been a lot of discussion. Opener has made an opening bid; responder has replied. Opener has made a rebid, giving a further description of the hand. In most cases, responder now knows enough about the combined strength and distribution to make the final decision for the partnership. That's usually the best idea—before everyone gets indigestion!

When considering responder's rebid, I could introduce detailed charts of what to bid with each type of hand, but I'd rather focus on concepts. In most auctions, you add what you know about opener's strength and distribution to what you see in your own hand, and make a decision about the contract. Keep focused on the goal of the bidding conversation. You want to get to the best bonus level the partnership can afford.

Responder places the strength of the hand into one of three categories—like the *Three Little Pigs* (just kidding!):

6–10 points	a minimum strength response
11–12 points	a medium strength response
13 or more points	a maximum strength response

Let's take a look at how you handle each type of hand.

Responder Has 6–10 Points

With 6–10 points, responder focuses on getting the partnership to the best contract. If opener shows a minimum-strength hand, this will be a partscore. If opener shows a medium-strength or maximum-strength hand, responder should be aiming higher.

Opener Shows a Minimum-Strength Hand

If opener could have as few as 13 points, and responder as few as 6, the partnership doesn't want to get too high. Responder wants to stop in the best partscore, and can do so in one of three ways:

- Passing—if the partnership is already in the best partscore.
- Returning to a previously bid suit.
- Bidding 1NT.

Suppose partner opens the bidding 1♦, and this is your hand:

♠ Q 10 8 6 4 3
♥ J 8
♦ Q 7 3
♣ J 4

Opener could have anywhere from 13 to 21 points, and could have a balanced or an unbalanced hand. Since it's too early to decide where the partnership belongs, you start by making a response of 1♠, showing your long suit. This is a forcing bid, and opener must make a rebid. Let's suppose the auction starts off this way:

OPENER	RESPONDER (YOU)
1♦	1♠
1NT	?

Opener is showing a minimum balanced hand, with no voids, and no singletons. Opener must have at least two spades. You've found an eight-card suit. Rebid 2♠, returning to a previously bid suit. This isn't forcing, and shows a hand in the 6–10 point range. Opener is expected to pass.

You have the same hand, and the auction starts off this way:

OPENER	RESPONDER (YOU)
1♦	1♠
2♠	?

Opener is again showing a minimum-strength hand, this time with support for your suit. You're already in the best partscore, so you can pass.

Now the auction proceeds in this manner:

OPENER	RESPONDER (YOU)
1♦	1♠
2♦	?

Opener didn't support your suit, didn't bid notrump, and didn't show a second suit. Opener is showing a minimum unbalanced hand with a long diamond suit. The hand belongs in partscore, and it looks as though the best trump fit is diamonds. Partner may not have any spades. Pass, and let partner play the hand with diamonds as trump.

Finally, the auction starts off this way:

OPENER	RESPONDER (YOU)
1♦	1♠
2♣	?

Opener hasn't shown any extra strength, but has shown an unbalanced hand with two suits. Opener is giving you a choice of trump suit. You could insist on playing with your spades as trump, but you don't mind diamonds. Rebid 2♦, returning to opener's first suit. This is called *giving preference*. You don't show any extra strength by going back to opener's first suit. You simply prefer diamonds to clubs as the trump suit. If you preferred clubs, you could pass.

Let's try a different hand for responder:

OPENER	RESPONDER (YOU)
1♦	1♥
1♠	?

♠ 10 3
♥ K J 8 6 2
♦ 9 6
♣ K 10 3 2

Opener has shown two suits, and you don't have support for either one. Opener didn't support your heart suit, and may not have very many hearts. Rebid 1NT. That looks like the best partscore. With a hand in the 6–10 point range, you shouldn't go venturing off into 2♣, introducing a fourth suit. That would be a forcing bid, and opener would have to bid again, perhaps getting the partnership too high.

Your 1NT rebid is not a sign-off bid; it merely suggests where you think the partnership belongs, and limits your hand to 6–10 points. Opener will often accept your decision and pass, but opener could have a very unbalanced hand such as this:

♠ K Q 8 4
♥ 7 5
♦ A Q J 8 5 2
♣ 4

With this hand, opener would go back to 2♦ after your 1NT rebid, and the partnership would end up in the best partscore.

Although opener hasn't shown any extra strength with the rebid of 1♠, opener could have a medium-strength hand. If that's the case, opener can show the extra strength after your 1NT rebid.

Opener Shows a Medium-Strength Hand

If opener does show a medium-strength hand of 17 or 18 points, responder decides whether the partnership belongs in partscore or game. If responder is at the bottom of the range, with 6 or 7 points, there won't be enough combined strength for a game level contract, and responder should stop in partscore. If responder is at the top of the range, with 9 or 10 points, there should be enough combined strength for a game contract. And, if responder has 8 points . . . ? This is where your judgment comes in: if you like your hand, bid game; if not, stop in partscore.

Let's see how this works in practice. Suppose the auction starts this way:

OPENER	RESPONDER (YOU)
1♦	1♥
3♥	?

Opener is showing a medium-strength hand by supporting your suit with a jump rather than raising to 2♥.

♠ J 10 8 4
♥ Q J 9 3
♦ 7 4
♣ K 4 2

If this is your hand as responder, you would pass. There are only 7 HCPs. Even if opener has 18 points, there's not enough combined strength for a game contract. Stop in partscore.

♠ 8 4
♥ A 10 8 6 3
♦ Q 5
♣ K 8 6 2

With this hand, you would accept the invitation, and go on to 4♥. You're at the top of the range, and even if opener has only 17 points, the partnership belongs at the game level.

Here's another auction:

	OPENER	RESPONDER (YOU)
	1♦	1♥
	3♦	?

By jumping to 3♦ rather than rebidding 2♦, opener is showing a hand of medium strength, 17–18 points.

♠ Q J 3
♥ A 10 8 4
♦ 7 4
♣ K 9 4 2

10 points, accept the invitation and bid game. Choose 3NT, rather than 5♦, since you're more likely to be able to take 9 tricks than 11 tricks, even with a fit in diamonds.

♠ Q J 3
♥ A J 8 4
♦ 7 4
♣ 10 9 4 2

With 8 points, you're on the borderline. The more conservative players would pass, leaving partner to play partscore in diamonds. The aggressive responders would try 3NT, hoping to find a way to take nine tricks. You may not know which is the better decision until the hand is over.

Opener can also show a hand of at least medium strength by making a reverse—bidding a second suit at the two level that's higher-ranking than the first. For example, the auction might go this way:

	OPENER	RESPONDER (YOU)
	1♦	1♠
	2♥	?

Most partnerships play that a reverse is forcing, and responder must bid again, although some partnerships allow responder to pass with only 6 or 7 points. If you haven't discussed this type of sequence with your partner, do what comes naturally. For example, suppose this is your hand:

♠ K 10 9 6 5 2
♥ 6 4
♦ J 5
♣ J 9 3

You don't have support for either of partner's suits, so rebid 2♠ to show the extra length in your suit. Let opener decide what to do next. Suppose you have this hand:

♠ K Q 9 6
♥ J 4
♦ Q 9 2
♣ 10 8 6 3

Bid 3♦, giving preference back to partner's first suit. With only a medium-strength hand, partner can pass. With a maximum-strength hand, partner can bid to game.

Recognizing a reverse and handling the subsequent auction is one of the more challenging aspects of bidding.

Opener Shows a Maximum-Strength Hand

With 6–10 points after opener shows a maximum-strength hand of 19–21 points, the partnership is committed to the game level. Responder makes sure that the partnership gets to the best game level contract. For example, suppose the auction proceeds in this manner:

OPENER	RESPONDER (YOU)
1♥	2♥
4♥	?

By going to the game level after your raise to 2♥, opener is showing a maximum-strength hand. It doesn't matter what your hand is, the partnership is already at the game level. There's nothing left to do but pass.

On the other hand, suppose the auction starts off this way:

OPENER	RESPONDER (YOU)
1♠	1NT
3♥	?

Opener's jump shift shows a maximum-strength hand, and the partnership is committed to the game level. The auction is not over, however, since the partnership has not yet agreed on the best contract. You'll have to help partner decide by making a suitable rebid based on the nature of your hand.

♠ 5 2
♥ Q 6
♦ K 9 8 6 3
♣ Q J 9 2

With this hand, you don't have support for either of partner's suits. Choose 3NT. Partner will likely leave the contract there unless partner's hand is very unbalanced.

♠ 10 8
♥ K 9 6 4
♦ Q 8 3
♣ Q 9 6 4

Choose 4♥. You prefer partner's second suit as the trump suit. You can't pass and leave the partnership in partscore because opener is showing a maximum-strength hand.

Responder Has 11–12 Points

With 11–12 points, responder tries to get the partnership to the game level, even if opener has a minimum-strength hand. If opener shows a medium-strength or maximum-strength hand, the partnership should always end up at the game level.

Opener Shows a Minimum-Strength Hand

When responder has 11 or 12 points, the partnership is close to having the combined strength for a game contract. Only if opener has a meagre 13 or 14 points for the opening bid will the partnership rest in partscore. Responder wants to move toward game without actually bidding it—leaving room for opener to pass with 13 or

14 points, but encouraging opener to continue with more. Responder can do this in a couple of ways:

- Bidding 2NT.
- Bidding a previously bid suit at the three level.

To see how this works, let's suppose partner opens the bidding 1♦, and this is your hand:

♠ 8 4 3
♥ K Q 10 6
♦ J 8
♣ A J 10 4

You respond 1♥, looking for a fit by bidding up the line. Partner rebids 1♠, and now it's up to you.

OPENER	RESPONDER (YOU)
1♦	1♥
1♠	?

You have a balanced hand with 11 HCPs. That's too much to rebid 1NT, which would show a hand in the 6–10 point category. On the other hand, it isn't enough to go all the way to 3NT since partner may have only 13 or 14 points. Instead, you compromise by bidding 2NT, moving toward game without actually bidding it. This is an invitational bid. With a little extra strength, partner can bid game. Otherwise, partner can pass.

The situation would be similar if the auction goes this way:

OPENER	RESPONDER (YOU)
1♦	1♥
1NT	?

Raise to 2NT. Partner has shown a balanced hand too weak to open 1NT, and there's no eight-card major suit fit. Move toward game, asking if opener has a little extra. If not, the partnership will rest in partscore.

Suppose the auction starts in this manner:

OPENER	RESPONDER (YOU)
1♦	1♥
2♥	?

By raising to the two level, partner has shown support for your suit, but only a minimum-strength hand. You have too much to pass, but not enough to commit the partnership to game. You can take the middle ground by bidding 3♥. With a little extra, partner can move on to game. Otherwise, partner can pass.

Some partnerships might bid 3♣ with this hand, rather than 3♥. This is referred to as a *game try*, since responder is trying for game by showing another feature of the hand. Unless your partnership has discussed the meanings of such bids, it's easier to use the 1♥–2♥–3♥ approach—simple, but effective. You're bidding a previously bid suit, hearts, at the three level to show an invitational hand.

Incidentally, that reminds me of the story of a partnership who said they used the 1–2–3 approach. They bid one, should have bid two, and went down three! Hopefully, your partnership will have a little more luck.

The auction could start like this:

OPENER	RESPONDER (YOU)
1♦	1♥
2♣	?

With your support for partner's second suit, raise to 3♣. Again, you're bidding a suit at the three level which has previously been bid by the partnership. This shows an invitational hand of 11–12 points. Opener can pass or go on to game.

Let's try a different hand:

♠ 10 5
♥ A Q 10 9 6 3 2
♦ Q 10
♣ 8 5

The auction starts:

OPENER	RESPONDER (YOU)
1♦	1♥
1NT	?

Your hand is worth 11 points—8 HCPs plus three for the seven-card suit. That's too much to simply rebid 2♥. Partner would assume that you have a hand in the 6–10 point range, and that you want to play in partscore. Bid 3♥. This is invitational, since it's a three-level bid of a suit previously bid by the partnership.

With this hand, you would make the same second bid if partner were to rebid 1♠, 2♣, 2♦, or 2♥. Some hands are easier than others.

Suppose you were to pick up this hand, and partner opens the bidding 1♥:

> ♠ 9 4
> ♥ K 8 5
> ♦ Q J 2
> ♣ K Q 10 6 3

We've encountered this type of hand when talking about responder's first bid. You have the strength for a limit raise of partner's suit, but only three-card support. An immediate jump to 3♥ should show four-card support for opener's suit. Instead of raising right away, you start by bidding a new suit, and the auction might proceed in this manner:

OPENER	RESPONDER (YOU)
1♥	2♣
2♥	?

Now you bid 3♥. This is another example of bidding a suit at the three level that's previously been bid by the partnership to show an invitational hand of 11–12 points.

Opener Shows a Medium-Strength Hand

If opener has a medium-strength hand of 17 or 18 points, and responder has 11 or 12 points, you're going to the game level. The partnership has at least 28 combined points—enough for game—and at most 30 points—not enough for slam.

Suppose you have this hand:

> ♠ K J 8 3
> ♥ Q 8 4
> ♦ 10 2
> ♣ K Q 8 2

The auction starts off in this manner:

OPENER	RESPONDER (YOU)
1♦	1♠
3♠	?

By raising your suit with a jump, opener is showing a medium-strength hand of 17–18 points with support for your suit. Bid 4♠. There should be plenty of strength for game, but it's unlikely the partnership can take the twelve tricks required for a slam contract.

Similarly, suppose the auction started like this:

OPENER	RESPONDER (YOU)
1♦	1♠
3♦	?

Bid 3NT. There's no eight-card major suit fit, and it should be easier to take nine tricks rather than the eleven tricks needed to make 5♦.

You would also bid 3NT if opener showed a medium-strength hand with this type of auction:

OPENER	RESPONDER (YOU)
1♦	1♠
2♥	?

Opener has shown extra strength by bidding a suit at the two level that's higher-ranking than opener's first suit—a reverse. Without support for either of opener's suits and with lots of strength in the other two suits, 3NT should be the best contract.

Opener Shows a Maximum-Strength Hand

If opener shows a maximum-strength hand of about 19–21 points, the target is still the game level when responder has 11–12 points. On rare occasions when opener has 21 points, and responder has exactly 12 points, the partnership might miss a slam contract with 33 combined points. Otherwise, game will be just fine.

For example, suppose you pick up the following hand:

> ♠ Q J 8 5 3
> ♥ K 8 3
> ♦ J 4
> ♣ K 9 2

The auction starts off:

OPENER	RESPONDER (YOU)
1♦	1♠
4♠	?

By raising all the way to the game level, opener is showing a maximum-strength hand of 19–21 points. You have 10 HCPs plus 1 for the fifth spade. That should make you very comfortable in your game contract, and you should pass. There's not enough combined strength to venture toward the slam level.

Suppose the auction starts this way:

OPENER	RESPONDER (YOU)
1♦	1♠
3♣	?

Bid 3NT. Opener's jump shift into a new suit at the three level shows a maximum-strength hand. Based on the information you have, 3NT looks like the best contract for the partnership.

Responder Has 13 or More Points

If partner opens the bidding, and you have 13 or more points, you know the contract should be at least at the game level. Opener has 13 points, and you have 13 or more points. That gives the partnership at least 26 combined points. An opening bid opposite an opening bid produces a game. As responder, you're responsible for making sure the partnership doesn't rest below the game level. If you have 13 or more points, and opener shows a medium-strength or maximum-strength hand, the slam level starts to become the target.

Opener Shows a Minimum-Strength Hand

Although you know the partnership is headed for the game level when you have 13 or more points and partner opens the bidding, you can't settle on the contract right away. Opener can have a wide range of strength and distribution. You need to wait until you've heard partner's rebid before making a decision. For example, suppose partner opens the bidding 1♥, and this is your hand:

> ♠ A J 8 4
> ♥ K 5
> ♦ 10 8 4
> ♣ K Q J 3

Without support for partner's suit, you start by bidding 1♠. A new suit by responder is forcing, and you wait to hear opener's rebid. Suppose the auction continues in this manner:

OPENER	RESPONDER (YOU)
1♥	1♠
2♠	?

Partner is showing support for your suit and a minimum-strength hand. The partnership has found its major suit fit, and there's enough combined strength for game. Rebid 4♠, putting the partnership in the best final contract.

Alternatively, the auction might proceed in this manner:

OPENER	RESPONDER (YOU)
1♥	1♠
1NT	?

Partner is showing a minimum balanced hand without support for your suit. Bid 3NT, putting the partnership in a game contract. With 14 HCPs, you have too much to make an invitational raise to 2NT, since opener might pass. You're the captain. Take control.

The auction might go this way:

OPENER	RESPONDER (YOU)
1♥	1♠
2♦	?

Opener is showing hearts and diamonds. You have spades and clubs. Rebid 3NT, putting the partnership in the best game contract.

Or, the auction could go like this:

OPENER	RESPONDER (YOU)
1♥	1♠
2♥	?

The opening bid showed at least a five-card heart suit. By rebidding the heart suit, opener is showing an unbalanced hand. Opener can't support your suit or show another suit, so you can infer that opener has at least a six-card suit. With your two-card support, there's an eight-card major suit fit, and the hand belongs at the game level. Rebid 4♥.

Opener Shows a Medium-Strength Hand

The partnership requires about 33 combined points to undertake a slam level contract. If opener shows a hand of medium strength, 17 or 18 points, responder should consider slam as the target level when holding 15 or more points. Responder should settle for game with 13 or 14 points.

For example, suppose partner opens the bidding 1♦, and this is your hand:

♠ K Q 10 5
♥ Q J 4
♦ 8 2
♣ A J 8 3

You respond 1♠, and the auction continues:

OPENER	RESPONDER (YOU)
1♦	1♠
3♦	?

Opener's jump to the three level shows a medium-strength hand. You have 13 HCPs. The partnership has enough for a game contract, but not enough for a slam contract, even if partner holds 18 points. Since there's no major suit fit, settle for 3NT.

On the other hand, suppose the auction goes the same way, and this is your hand:

♠ A K 8 7 5
♥ 7 3
♦ K 10 8
♣ K Q 3

Bid 6♦. Your hand is worth 15 HCPs plus 1 point for distribution. Partner has 17 or 18 points, so there are at least 33 combined points. With your support, diamonds should be a suitable trump suit. Bid what you think you can make. Time to go for that slam bonus!

Opener Shows a Maximum-Strength Hand

When responder has 13 or more points, and opener describes a maximum-strength hand of 19–21 points, it's definitely your chance to collect the extra reward for bidding a slam. For example, suppose you pick up this hand:

♠ K 9 4
♥ K Q 8 3
♦ A 10 5
♣ Q J 7

The bidding proceeds:

OPENER	RESPONDER (YOU)
1♣	1♥
2NT	?

By bidding one of a suit, and then jumping in notrump, opener is showing a hand too strong to open the bidding 1NT. Rebid 6NT. Your 15 HCPs combined with opener's 19–21 points gives the partnership enough for a slam contract.

Slam bidding will be discussed in more detail later in the book. For now, add up the points, and away you go!

Summary

If opener shows a minimum-strength hand of 13–16 points, use the following guidelines:

6–10 points	Pass—if the partnership is already in the best partscore. Return to a previously bid suit. Bid 1NT.
11–12 points	Bid 2NT. Bid a previously bid suit at the three level.
13 or more	Bid to the game level.

If opener shows a medium-strength hand of 17–18 points:

6–8 points	Stop in partscore.
9 or more	Bid to the game level.

If opener shows a maximum strength hand of 19–21 points:

6–14 points	Bid to the game level.
15 or more	Bid to the slam level.

Exercises

1. What would be your rebid with this hand in each of the following auctions?

♠ Q 9 5
♥ A 10 8 4
♦ Q J 2
♣ 9 4 2

a) OPENER   RESPONDER
     1♣   1♥
     1♠   ?

b) OPENER   RESPONDER
     1♣   1♥
   1NT   ?

c) OPENER   RESPONDER
     1♣   1♥
     2♣   ?

d) OPENER   RESPONDER
     1♣   1♥
     2♥   ?

e) OPENER   RESPONDER
     1♣   1♥
   2NT   ?

f) OPENER   RESPONDER
     1♣   1♥
     3♣   ?

g) OPENER   RESPONDER
     1♣   1♥
     3♥   ?

2. What would be your rebid with this hand in each of the following auctions?

♠ K J 8 5
♥ A 9
♦ K 10 9 3
♣ 10 8 2

a) OPENER   RESPONDER
   1♥   1♠
  1NT   ?

b) OPENER   RESPONDER
   1♥   1♠
   2♦   ?

c) OPENER   RESPONDER
   1♥   1♠
   2♥   ?

d) OPENER   RESPONDER
   1♥   1♠
   2♠   ?

e) OPENER   RESPONDER
   1♥   1♠
  2NT   ?

f) OPENER   RESPONDER
   1♥   1♠
   3♠   ?

g) OPENER   RESPONDER
   1♥   1♠
   4♥   ?

3. What would be your rebid with this hand in each of the following auctions?

♠ Q J 5
♥ A Q 8 2
♦ 9 3
♣ A J 8 2

a) OPENER   RESPONDER
    1♦   1♥
    1♠   ?

b) OPENER   RESPONDER
    1♦   1♥
   1NT   ?

c) OPENER   RESPONDER
    1♦   1♥
    2♦   ?

d) OPENER   RESPONDER
    1♦   1♥
    2♥   ?

e) OPENER   RESPONDER
    1♦   1♥
    3♣   ?

f) OPENER   RESPONDER
    1♦   1♥
    3♦   ?

g) OPENER   RESPONDER
    1♦   1♥
    4♥   ?

Answers to Exercises

1a) 1NT. Your hand falls in the 6–10 point range, and opener hasn't shown any extra strength or support for your suit. Put the partnership in the best partscore.

1b) Pass. Opener is showing a balanced hand too weak to open 1NT. With only 9 HCPs, leave partner in partscore.

1c) Pass. Partner's rebid shows a minimum-strength unbalanced hand with no second suit to show. Clubs should be the best trump suit.

1d) Pass. You've found a major suit fit, but partner's raise shows a minimum-strength hand. You're high enough.

1e) 3NT. Partner is showing a balanced hand too strong to open 1NT. There's enough combined strength for game, and there's no major suit fit.

1f) 3NT. Partner is showing a medium-strength hand, of 17–18 points. There's enough combined strength for game.

1g) 4♥. Partner is showing a medium-strength hand, and you're at the top of the 6–10 point range. Accept the invitation and continue on to game.

2a) 2NT. Partner has a minimum balanced hand without support for your suit. With 11 HCPs, raise to 2NT, inviting opener to bid game with a little extra strength. Opener can pass with only 13 or 14 points.

2b) 3♦. With support for partner's second suit, raise to the three level to show an invitational hand of 11–12 points.

2c) 3♥. Partner's rebid shows a minimum-strength hand with at least a six-card heart suit. Invite partner to carry on to game by raising a previously mentioned suit to the three level.

2d) 3♠. Partner has a minimum-strength hand with support for your suit. Go to the three level to invite partner to bid game with a little extra strength.

2e) 3NT. Partner is showing a balanced hand too strong to open the bidding 1NT. Your 11 HCPs plus partner's 19–21 points should be enough for game, but not enough for a slam contract.

2f) 4♠. Partner's rebid shows a medium-strength hand with support for your suit. There's enough combined strength for game in your eight-card major suit fit.

2g) Pass. Partner is showing a maximum-strength hand of 19–21 points with support for your suit. With only 11 HCPs, the partnership doesn't have the 33 combined points usually required for a slam level contract. Settle for game.

3a) 3NT. With 14 HCPs opposite an opening bid, the partnership belongs in a game contract. Opener hasn't supported your suit, and there doesn't appear to be an eight-card major suit fit. Take the partnership to the best game level contract.

3b) 3NT. Opener is showing a minimum-strength balanced hand. The partnership belongs in a game contract. As captain, it's your responsibility to place the contract.

3c) 3NT. Partner is showing a minimum-strength hand with a long diamond suit. Take the partnership to the most likely game contract.

3d) 4♥. The partnership has found a major suit fit, and there's enough combined strength for a game contract.

3e) 6♣. Opener's jump shift into a new suit shows a maximum-strength hand of 19–21 points. The partnership has the 33 combined points needed for a slam contract, and there's an eight-card fit in clubs. Time to go for the bonus. More sophisticated slam bidding techniques will be discussed in a later chapter.

3f) 3NT. Opener is describing a medium-strength hand with a long diamond suit. You have all the information you need to place the contract.

3g) 6♥. Opener has a maximum-strength hand with support for your heart suit. The partnership belongs at the slam level in the eight-card fit.

Part 5

WHEN
BOTH SIDES
HAVE SOMETHING
TO SAY

11

The Overcall

"Play bridge for fun. The instant you find you're playing for any other reason, go on to something else."

The auction is a conversation. So far in this bridge book, two people have been taking part in the conversation, the opener and the responder. The other pair at the table has been quiet. As you know, this isn't always the case. The next three chapters look at the bidding conversation when both sides are in the auction.

Since the members of the other partnership are going to be in the auction from this point on, they have to be identified. It's part of the game's vocabulary to refer to the other pair as the opponents. The player on your right is referred to as your right-hand opponent or RHO. The player on your left is referred to as your left-hand opponent or LHO. Now I have to tell you, I don't like the word "opponent." A look through my thesaurus doesn't help: enemy, rival, antagonist, foe.

This seems like a good time to share my thoughts on bridge as a competitive sport. Bridge is certainly a competitive sport at the level of the World Championships, where the aim is to defeat the other pairs and teams. To the vast majority of players, however, bridge is entertainment, and an opportunity for social contact. There are stories—some of them true, unfortunately—about players who sit down at the bridge table, and come away feeling defeated. They thought they were sitting down to pass time over a friendly game of cards. It turned out they were actually going into a battle. There are competitive bridge games, and there are social bridge games. Both have merit. Make sure you're playing in a game that suits your taste. In these chapters, I also refer to the other pair as opponents, but I mean it in the nicest of ways!

Suppose you're planning to open the bidding, but you aren't the dealer. Your right-hand opponent mentions a suit before you get a chance to bid. How inconvenient. Yet there are some advantages when an opponent opens the auction in front of you. Instead of the original bid you were planning to make, you now have three options: you can pass, make a bid, or say "double." The use of the double is discussed in the next chapter. In this chapter the focus is on the choice between bidding and passing.

The Simple Overcall

A bid of a suit or notrump after your opponents have started the auction, is referred to as an *overcall*—a call over the opponent's bid. For example, the bidding might start this way:

LEFT-HAND OPPONENT (LHO)	PARTNER	RIGHT-HAND OPPONENT (RHO)	YOU
		1♦	1♠

You've made an overcall of 1♠. An overcall made at the cheapest available level is referred to as a *simple overcall*. From partner's perspective, this overcall appears similar to an opening bid of 1♠. Overcalls and opening bids do have their similarities, but there can be differences as well. Suppose the bidding starts this way:

LEFT-HAND OPPONENT (LHO)	PARTNER	RIGHT-HAND OPPONENT (RHO)	YOU
		1♦	Pass
1♠	2♥		

Partner is making an overcall of 2♥. Right away you can see a contrast between opening the bidding and making an overcall. Partner can no longer open the bidding 1♥. To suggest hearts as the trump suit in this auction, partner has to start by bidding them at the two level. Competition for the contract makes a difference.

It would be convenient if the guidelines for making overcalls and responding to overcalls were exactly the same as those for opening the bidding and responding to opening bids. Overcalls, however, need to be viewed a little differently than opening bids.

The reason for opening the bidding is so that your side can have a constructive auction to reach the best contract. That's still a valid reason for making an overcall. Although the opponents have started the auction, there's no reason to believe that your side can't bid and make a contract. There are many hands on which you want to compete for the right to name the trump suit. The opponents feel they can take eight tricks with spades as the trump suit; you're willing to try to take nine tricks with hearts as the trump suit. That's what competition is all about.

There are, however, other reasons for entering the auction. By entering the auction with an overcall, you interfere with the smooth flow of conversation between the opponents. They no longer have things all their own way. You might make it difficult or impossible for them to exchange enough information to reach the best contract. They may bid too much or too little. Even if the opponents do end up winning the auction, your bidding will help your side to defend the contract, since you know something about each other's hand.

Let's see how all of this affects your decision to overcall when the opponents have opened the bidding.

Length and Strength

To open the bidding in a suit at the one level, you need about 13 or more points, and a five-card or longer major suit. You sometimes open a minor with a four-card, or even a three-card, suit to get the auction started while you search for your best spot. Once the opponents have started the auction, you should have **a five-card or longer suit to make an overcall**.

The opponents have shown some strength by opening the bidding, so there's some danger in competing. Partner may not have much of the remaining strength, and it would be easy for your side to get too high. The opponents could collect a bonus for defeating your contract. On the whole, the longer and stronger your suit, the safer it is to make an overcall.

The playing strength of a hand was discussed in the first chapter. Factors such as having your high cards together in your long suit, and holding 10's and 9's rather than small cards, can make a hand more valuable when it comes to taking tricks. Suppose the opponent on your right opens the bidding 1♣. Compare these two hands which you might hold:

	1)	♠ Q 5 4 3		2)	♠ K Q J 10 9
		♥ K Q			♥ A 5
		♦ Q 8 5 2			♦ 9 6 5
		♣ A 4 2			♣ 6 4 2

The first hand has 13 HCPs, and you would open the bidding 1♦. Once the bidding is opened in front of you, the situation is a little different. It would be quite dangerous to step into the auction by overcalling 1♦ or 1♠. Neither of your suits is very strong, and you would struggle to take more than two or three tricks if partner turns out to have very little strength and support for your suit.

The second hand is quite different. You have only 10 HCPs plus 1 for the fifth spade, and would probably not open the bidding with this hand. Nonetheless, this is a much better hand with which to overcall 1♠ when the opponent on your right opens 1♣. Even if partner has no support for your spade suit and no high cards, you should still end up taking four spade tricks, and the ♥A. Not too bad. By overcalling 1♠, you'll interfere with the opponents' auction. Your left-hand opponent can no longer bid 1♥. In addition, if your side ends up defending, you would like your partner to lead a spade to help establish tricks for your side. Finally, if partner does have a good hand with support for spades, your side can compete effectively for the contract.

Pass with the first hand. Overcall 1♠ with the second hand. You should have a good suit to make an overcall, usually five or more cards in length. If you don't have a good suit, you'll need extra strength to justify making an overcall.

That brings up an important point about competitive auctions.

Once the opponents have opened the bidding, **you don't have to bid just because you have 13 or more points**. If your hand is unsuitable for an overcall or, as will be explained in the next chapter, a double, you should pass, and await developments. There may be an opportunity to get into the auction later. Partner is still there.

Let's look at some examples of other hands you might hold after the auction is opened 1♣ on your right.

♠ 6 4
♥ A Q J 8 5
♦ K Q 6 2
♣ J 3

Overcall 1♥. You would have opened the bidding 1♥ with this hand, and the opponent's 1♣ bid doesn't prevent you from overcalling 1♥. You have both a good suit and a good hand, so an overcall is the best way to get into the auction.

♠ Q 6
♥ J 5 2
♦ A Q 10 8 7 3
♣ 10 3

Overcall 1♦. You wouldn't open the bidding at the one level with this hand, but with a decent six-card suit this is your opportunity to get into the auction. An overcall doesn't promise the values for an opening bid. It only sends the message that you have some length and strength in your suit, and would like to compete.

♠ K 9 7
♥ K 4 3
♦ A 5 3
♣ Q J 4 3

Pass. Although there are 13 HCPs, you don't have a suit to overcall. This isn't the right type of hand to compete for the contract at this point in the auction. You don't mind if the opponents want to play with clubs as trumps—that's your best suit!

♠ K J 9 6 4
♥ 8 5
♦ A K 10 7 3
♣ 3

Overcall 1♠. With a choice of five-card suits to bid, start with the higher-ranking.

♠ K 8   Pass. Although you have a five-card suit, it's
♥ 10 8 6 5 2   not a very good one. With only 9 HCPs, you
♦ K J 3   don't have the extra strength that would make
♣ Q 9 3   it worthwhile to get into the auction. Over-
                         calling 1♥ on this type of hand is liable to steer
the partnership in the wrong direction. You don't particularly want
partner to lead hearts if the opponents win the contract.

♠ 10 6   Overcall 1♥ (or pass). Although you don't
♥ A K Q 10   have a five-card suit to overcall, your hearts
♦ 9 7 3   are so strong you might make an exception
♣ K 8 4 2   here and treat them as a five-card suit. You
                         would certainly like partner to lead hearts if
the opponents end up playing the contract, and it's relatively safe to
enter the auction at this low level. You could also choose to pass if
that's your partnership style.

Watching the Level

Suppose you pick up this hand:

♠ Q J 3
♥ A 7
♦ Q 6 2
♣ K J 9 7 5

You're planning to open the bidding 1♣, but the dealer is on
your left, and the bidding proceeds:

LHO	PARTNER	RHO	YOU
1♠	Pass	2♦	?

You'd like to compete for the contract, but to show the club suit
you'd have to overcall 3♣, contracting to take nine of the thirteen
tricks. That's a dangerously high level at which to enter the bidding
with only 13 HCPs, and not a very strong five-card suit. Partner didn't
compete over 1♠, and the opponents likely have most of the missing

high cards. Better to go quietly with this hand, and try to defeat whatever contract the opponents reach.

While it's fairly safe to make an overcall at the one level, even with less than the values for an opening bid, the stakes increase when you have to start competing at the two level or higher. The opponents may decide that they can defeat your contract, and choose to defend. They may even double the contract to increase the value of the bonus they intend to receive for defeating you. The penalties for being defeated in a contract are outlined in the Scoring Summary in the Appendix—but you probably get the picture.

To make an overcall in a suit at the two level or higher, you should have a six-card suit, or a very good five-card suit, and the equivalent of an opening bid or better. The higher the overcall, the longer your suit should be, and the stronger your hand. Let's look at some examples after the bidding is opened 1♠ on your right.

♠ 8
♥ A K J 10 8 5
♦ 7 3
♣ K Q 7 3

Overcall 2♥. This is certainly a sound two-level overcall. You have an excellent suit, and more than the values for an opening bid. You should probably overcall with this hand even if you had to do so at the three level.

♠ Q 10 6
♥ K 8
♦ K Q 9 7 5
♣ 9 5 4

Pass. You might overcall 1♦ if the opening bid were 1♣, but it's too dangerous to introduce a mediocre five-card suit at the two level with only 10 HCPs. You don't have to compete for every contract!

♠ 6
♥ A Q 9 6 4
♦ 7 3
♣ A J 10 8 5

Overcall 2♥. You only have 11 HCPs, and your suit isn't that strong, but there's some measure of safety in having a reasonable second suit. If partner has no support for hearts, you might find a safe landing spot in clubs.

There's no guarantee that you'll be successful on this type of hand, but you do want to compete whenever possible. Don't sit back and let the opponents have a free rein.

Feeling Vulnerable

In addition to watching the level at which you must overcall, it's also a good idea to keep an eye on the vulnerability. Scoring and vulnerability are covered in more detail in the first book of this series, *Basics*, and there's a summary at the back of the book. Suffice it to say that the points lost for failing to fulfill your contract are twice as much when you're vulnerable—100 points, rather than 50 points, for each trick you're defeated—and can be much larger if the contract is doubled for penalties by the opponents.

If your decision is close on whether or not to overcall, be more conservative when your side is vulnerable. You can be more aggressive in the bidding when nonvulnerable. For example, suppose this is your hand when the opponent on your right opens the bidding 1♦:

> ♠ Q 10 8 6 5
> ♥ 10 5
> ♦ K J 3
> ♣ Q 6 3

Although you might risk a 1♠ overcall to try to compete when your side is not vulnerable, it wouldn't be a good idea if your side is vulnerable. The penalty could be quite severe if partner doesn't have much help for you. Time to exercise some caution.

Playing Their Song

What about overcalling in the same suit that the opponents have bid? Don't do it! Suppose the opponent on your right opens the bidding 1♦, and this is your hand:

> ♠ K 9 3
> ♥ 8 7
> ♦ A K J 8 5
> ♣ Q 6 2

The opponent on your right is currently contracting to take seven tricks with diamonds as the trump suit. It wouldn't be a good idea for you to bid 2♦, and try to make eight tricks with diamonds as trump. Instead, pass quietly. You're happy to defend if the opponents want to play in your best suit.

Since it's unlikely that you'll want to play in a suit bid by the opponents, a bid of the opponent's suit is referred to as a *cue bid*, and usually carries a special message. A direct overcall in the opponent's suit is commonly used to show a very strong hand, usually with the ability to win the first trick in that suit. It shows a hand too strong for a simple overcall, the type of hand that you were planning to open at the two level to show about 22 or more points. For example, if the opening bid were 1♦, you might bid 2♦ with this sort of hand:

♠ A K Q 10 8 6
♥ A K J 10
♦ A
♣ 6 2

You're too strong for a simple overcall of 1♠, which partner could pass.

Cue bids of the opponent's suit can be assigned other meanings. It's best to discuss this with partner before trying it out. The next chapter will discuss another way of showing such a strong hand.

Responding to an Overcall

Responding to an overcall is similar to responding to an opening bid. An overcall at the one level might contain less than the values for an opening bid, but you can assume partner has a five-card or longer suit, even if the overcall is in diamonds or clubs.

The Overcaller's Message

The message of an overcall is similar to that of an opening bid. It's an invitational bid, and you can pass if it seems unlikely that the partnership belongs any higher than partscore. If there's the possibility that your side can make a game contract, however, you should bid. Even if partner is trying to compete for the contract, and has less than the values for an opening bid, you want to get into the act whenever you can.

The general approach is to treat partner's overcall as though it shows an opening bid or better, especially when the overcall is at the two level or higher. You can pass, support partner's suit, bid a new suit, or bid notrump. When the opponents open the bidding in a suit, you have one additional option. You can bid the opponent's suit. Let's look at each of your options in turn.

Passing the Overcall

With 0–5 points, you should pass, as you would if partner were opening the bidding. You can't afford to get the partnership too high. With 6 or more points, you want to try to make a bid, since partner could have a very good hand.

Some partnerships limit the upper range of a simple overcall to about 16 points, allowing responder to pass with 9 or fewer points. Even if this isn't your partnership style, you don't have to stretch to respond with only 6 or 7 points when partner makes a simple overcall at the one level, and you have no support. Partner could have less than the values for an opening bid, and you want to be cautious about getting the partnership overboard.

For example, suppose the auction starts in this manner:

LHO	PARTNER	RHO	YOU
1♦	1♥	Pass	?

♠ Q 8 7 6
♥ 9 6 4
♦ J 7 3
♣ J 8 5

Pass. This would be the same action you would take if partner had opened the bidding 1♥.

♠ J 9 7 6
♥ 6 4
♦ J 6 2
♣ K J 5 2

Pass. Although you have 6 HCPs, and should respond 1♠ if partner opened the bidding 1♥, there's less reason to bid when partner simply overcalls at the one level. Any bid you make is unlikely to improve the contract, and may get your side into difficulty if partner has less than opening bid values for the 1♥ overcall.

If your right-hand opponent were to bid rather than pass, you don't have to bid on a hand with 6 or more points. With a very strong hand, partner will get another opportunity to bid in the auction. This shouldn't stop you from bidding, however, if you do have something to say. Partner is trying to compete, and you want to work together.

You also tend to pass with about 6–8 points when partner makes an overcall at the two level. There's no room left to bid a new suit at the one level, to bid 1NT, or to raise to the two level. Passing will usually work out best.

Supporting Partner

Since partner will usually have a good five-card or longer suit, you can support partner's suit with three or more cards. When raising partner, you can use the following approach, which has a familiar ring:

6–10 points	Raise one level
11–12 points	Raise by jumping a level
13 or more points	Raise to the game level

There are some other approaches that can be used with 11 or more points which will be discussed later, but this approach is what we will use for now. For example, suppose the bidding starts this way:

LHO	PARTNER	RHO	YOU
1♣	1♠	Pass	?

♠ K J 6
♥ K 8 2
♦ J 9 7 6 3
♣ 10 8

Raise to 2♠. You have three-card support for partner's suit and 8 HCPs, plus 1 for distribution. You would make the same response if partner opened the bidding 1♠.

♠ Q 9 6 3
♥ K 2
♦ A J 9 7
♣ J 10 8

Bid 3♠. This is a limit raise showing good support, and about 11–12 points. Partner can pass with 14 or fewer points, but continue on to game with more.

♠ A J 9 5 3   Bid 4♠. You have 11 HCPs, and can count 3
♥ 2   dummy points for the singleton heart. That's
♦ K J 8 5 3   enough to raise partner to the game level.
♣ Q 8   Partner might have less than an opening bid
                     for the overcall, but with a little luck, you'll
still make the contract.

Bidding a New Suit

If partner opens the bidding, a response of a new suit is a forcing
bid, and opener is expected to bid again. You can use a similar approach when responding to an overcall. Suppose the bidding starts
in this manner:

LHO	PARTNER	RHO	YOU
1♦	1♥	Pass	?

♠ A Q J 7 3   Respond 1♠. You don't have support for
♥ 8 2   partner's suit, but you have too much strength
♦ 9 6 4   to pass. If partner has some extra strength,
♣ A 7 3   there may be enough combined strength for
                     a game contract. There may also be a better
spot to play the hand than in partner's heart suit. By bidding 1♠ you
can get further information from partner to help decide where the
partnership belongs.

♠ A 9 4   Respond 2♣. As when responding to an
♥ Q 3   opening bid, you should have 11 or more
♦ 9 4   points to introduce a new suit at the two level.
♣ K Q 10 8 6 4

Some partnerships prefer to treat a new suit as nonforcing after
an overcall. This requires extensive use of the cue bid, as discussed
later, to show good hands. I'd suggest that you don't adopt this style
unless you've discussed all the ramifications with your partner be-
forehand. Treat a new suit by the responder to the overcall as a forcing bid.

Bidding Notrump

Notrump responses to partner's overcall are similar to notrump responses to an opening bid. For example, a 1NT response tells partner that you have about 6–10 points without support for partner's suit, and without a suit to show at the one level. Since the opponents are likely to lead the suit they've bid, you should also have some strength in the opponent's suit to bid notrump.

Suppose the bidding starts this way:

LHO	PARTNER	RHO	YOU
1♥	1♠	Pass	?

♠ J 6
♥ A J 10
♦ J 8 6 3
♣ Q 10 7 3

Respond 1NT. You don't have three-card support for partner's suit, and can't bid a new suit at the one level. You do have 9 HCPs, and some strength in the opponent's heart suit. 1NT will keep the bidding going in case partner has a strong hand.

♠ Q 10
♥ A Q 8 2
♦ J 10 6 5
♣ K 9 3

Respond 2NT. Following the limit bid approach, this is an invitational bid showing about 11–12 points. Partner can pass with nothing extra, or continue on to game with a good hand.

The Cue Bid

As discussed earlier, it's not a good idea to bid the suit bid by the opponents with the intention of playing with that suit as trump. Bidding the opponents' suit usually carries some special message, and is referred to as a cue bid.

Cue bidding the opponents' suit in response to an overcall by partner is generally played as an artificial, forcing bid, asking the overcaller to further describe the hand. After hearing the overcaller's rebid, responder can then decide what to do next.

The cue bid is used in different ways depending on the partnership style. If the partnership has an agreement that a new suit isn't forcing in response to an overcall, for example, then responder is left with only the cue bid to send a forcing message. Some partnerships treat the cue bid as forcing for only one round of the auction; others treat it as a commitment that the partnership is going to the game level.

You can get by without using the cue bid by simply making natural bids in response to an overcall as discussed above. If you want to start using this refinement, be sure to discuss it with your partner first.

Here's an example of how the cue bid might be used in a typical overcall situation. Suppose this is the beginning of the auction:

LHO	PARTNER	RHO	YOU
1♦	1♠	Pass	?

You have the following hand:

♠ K 4
♥ A Q 7 5
♦ Q 9 3 2
♣ K 8 6

You have 14 HCPs in response to partner's overcall, and the partnership belongs in a game contract unless partner has considerably less than opening bid values for the overcall. To get a further description of partner's hand, you could bid 2♦ at this point. This isn't an attempt to play in diamonds, merely a forcing bid—a cue bid of the opponent's suit. If partner rebids 2♥ to show a second suit, you can raise to 4♥. If partner rebids 2NT, showing a balanced hand with some strength in diamonds, you can raise to 3NT. If partner rebids 2♠, showing only a long spade suit and nothing much extra, you could raise spades or bid notrump at this point. Exactly how much you bid depends on how weak a hand your partner can have to make a one level overcall.

Your partnership may not want to get involved in the complications associated with using the cue bid. You could, instead, make a natural response with this hand, such as jumping in notrump, and you'll likely end up in the best contract. The only reason for introducing the cue bid at this point is to make you aware that it exists. It may come up when you're playing with a new partner or your opponents might use this bidding tool. To follow the auction, you'll need to know what's going on.

Overcalling in Notrump

You can treat an overcall in notrump in exactly the same manner as an opening bid of 1NT. There are, however, a couple of points you might want to keep in mind.

1NT Overcall

An overcall of 1NT describes the same sort of hand as an opening bid of 1NT. You should have a balanced hand with a limited range of strength, such as 16–18 points.

One consideration is that you should have some strength in the suit bid by your opponents. The opponents are likely to lead the suit bid by their side. You don't want them taking too many tricks before you have an opportunity to establish tricks for your side. For example, suppose this is your hand:

♠ 10 4
♥ A J 10 6
♦ A Q 9 5
♣ K Q 8

You would open the bidding 1NT with this hand, since it's balanced and contains 16 HCPs. If the opponent on your right opens the bidding 1♣, 1♦, or 1♥ you should overcall 1NT with this hand. You're describing the same type of hand to partner, and you have some strength in the suit the opponents have bid.

If the opponent's opening bid is 1♠, however, this is not such an ideal hand for a 1NT overcall because you don't have any length or strength in the spade suit. The opponents may take the first five or six spade tricks before you even get an opportunity to start taking your tricks. In the next chapter, you'll encounter a different way of competing which you could use in this situation.

Responding to a 1NT Overcall

If your partner overcalls 1NT, you can respond using methods similar to those that were discussed in Chapter 5:

- 0–7 points   Bid 2♣, 2♦, 2♥, or 2♠ with a five-card or longer suit. These are sign-off bids. Otherwise, pass.
- 8–9 points   Bid 2NT. This is an invitational bid.
- 10–14 points   Bid 4♥ or 4♠ with a six-card or longer suit. These are sign-off bids.

                                   Bid 3♥ or 3♠ with a five-card suit. These are forcing bids.

                                   Otherwise, bid 3NT. This is a sign-off bid.

The only difference is that any suit at the two level, other than the suit bid by the opponents, is a sign-off bid. If you (cue) bid the suit that the opponents opened, that takes the place of the 2♣ Stayman response, which will be discussed in a later chapter.

The 2NT Overcall

To keep things simple, your partnership can treat an overcall of 2NT over the opponent's one level bid in a suit in the same manner as an opening bid of 2NT. It could show a balanced hand of 22–24 points, and partner can take it from there.

You won't hold many hands with 22–24 points when the opponents open the bidding, and many partnerships prefer to assign a completely different meaning to the 2NT overcall. The *unusual 2NT overcall* is discussed in the chapter covering conventions.

The 3NT Overcall

As with the overcall of 2NT, it won't be often that you encounter a balanced hand with 25–27 points after the opponents open the bidding. You can use an overcall of 3NT to show this type of hand, but most partnerships prefer to adopt a slightly different use for this bid.

Suppose the opponent on your right opens the bidding 1♥, and you hold this hand:

♠ A 5
♥ A 2
♦ A K Q 10 8 6 5
♣ 6 4

You don't have a balanced hand with 25–27 points, but an over-call of 3NT is reasonable with this hand. If the opponents lead a heart, you expect to take nine tricks: the ♠A, ♥A, and seven dia-mond tricks. Of course, the opponents might surprise you by lead-ing a club and taking the first five club tricks, or the diamond suit might divide badly, and you end up with only five tricks. Because of the risk involved, this type of bid is referred to as a *gambling 3NT overcall*. Some partnerships use a similar style when opening the bid-ding 3NT.

Your partnership doesn't have to use the 3NT bid in this manner, but it's not a bad tactic to consider! You also don't want to be caught off-guard if your opponents favor this approach.

Jump Overcalls

Instead of making a simple overcall at the cheapest available level, you could jump in your suit. For example:

LHO	PARTNER	RHO	YOU
		1♥	2♠

Your bid of 2♠ is referred to as a *jump overcall*, since you could have made a simple overcall of 1♠. Although the time-honored use for this bid was to show a hand too strong for a simple overcall, most modern partnerships prefer to use this to show a weak hand with a long spade suit. The use of jump overcalls will be discussed in more detail in a later chapter.

Summary

When the opponents open the bidding, one way for your side to compete for the contract is by making an overcall. A simple overcall in a suit tends to show:

- A five-card or longer suit.
- Approximately the values for an opening bid.

Nonvulnerable overcalls at the one level are sometimes made with less than the values for an opening bid, but the higher the level, the more strength is required.

A 1NT overcall shows:

- A balanced hand.
- 16–18 points.
- Strength in the opponent's suit.

When responding to partner's overcall, you can use the same approach as when responding to an opening bid. The only difference is that an extra bid, the "cue" bid of the opponents' suit, is now available. It can be used by the partnership as a forcing response to get more information from partner. Partnership styles tend to vary depending on how much use is made of the cue bid. If in doubt, respond naturally, and the partnership should reach the right contract.

Exercises

1. What would you bid with each of the following hands after the auction starts:

LHO	PARTNER	RHO	YOU
		1♦	?

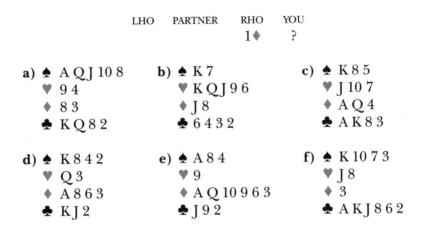

a) ♠ A Q J 10 8
  ♥ 9 4
  ♦ 8 3
  ♣ K Q 8 2

b) ♠ K 7
  ♥ K Q J 9 6
  ♦ J 8
  ♣ 6 4 3 2

c) ♠ K 8 5
  ♥ J 10 7
  ♦ A Q 4
  ♣ A K 8 3

d) ♠ K 8 4 2
  ♥ Q 3
  ♦ A 8 6 3
  ♣ K J 2

e) ♠ A 8 4
  ♥ 9
  ♦ A Q 10 9 6 3
  ♣ J 9 2

f) ♠ K 10 7 3
  ♥ J 8
  ♦ 3
  ♣ A K J 8 6 2

2. What would you respond to partner's overcall with each of the following hands after the auction starts:

LHO	PARTNER	RHO	YOU
1♣	1♥	· Pass	?

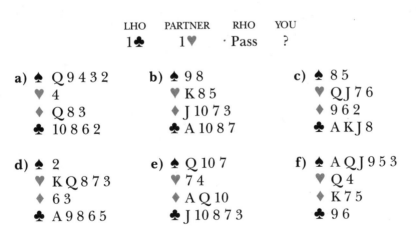

a) ♠ Q 9 4 3 2
  ♥ 4
  ♦ Q 8 3
  ♣ 10 8 6 2

b) ♠ 9 8
  ♥ K 8 5
  ♦ J 10 7 3
  ♣ A 10 8 7

c) ♠ 8 5
  ♥ Q J 7 6
  ♦ 9 6 2
  ♣ A K J 8

d) ♠ 2
  ♥ K Q 8 7 3
  ♦ 6 3
  ♣ A 9 8 6 5

e) ♠ Q 10 7
  ♥ 7 4
  ♦ A Q 10
  ♣ J 10 8 7 3

f) ♠ A Q J 9 5 3
  ♥ Q 4
  ♦ K 7 5
  ♣ 9 6

3. What would you respond to partner's overcall with each of the following hands after the auction starts:

LHO	PARTNER	RHO	YOU
1♥	1NT	Pass	?

a) ♠ 9 8 5 3
   ♥ J 4
   ♦ K 7 6 2
   ♣ 10 8 5

b) ♠ J 10 8 6 5 4
   ♥ 8 5
   ♦ 10 6 2
   ♣ J 5

c) ♠ K Q 8
   ♥ 6 4
   ♦ J 8 3
   ♣ A 10 9 6 5

Answers to Exercises

1a) 1♠. You would open the bidding 1♠ with this hand, and the opponents' bidding doesn't prevent you from sending the same message to partner.

1b) 1♥. Although you wouldn't open the bidding with this hand, you should seize the opportunity to make a one-level overcall. This may help the partnership to compete for the contract, and may help partner to find the best opening lead if your side ends up defending.

1c) 1NT. Make the same bid you would have made had the opponents not opened the bidding. You have some strength in their suit in case they lead it while defending.

1d) Pass. Although you have 13 points, you don't have a good five-card suit to overcall. Pass, and await developments.

1e) Pass. Although you were planning to open the bidding 1♦, the opponents have beaten you to the punch. You're happy to defend if this turns out to be the contract. Most partnerships don't use a bid of 2♦ in this situation as a natural overcall.

1f) 2♣. With a choice of suits, bid your long suit first. You may get an opportunity to show your spade suit later in the auction.

2a) Pass. With only 4 HCPs plus 1 point for the fifth spade, you don't have enough to respond. Even though 1♥ may not be the best contract for your side, if you bid, you may end up in a worse spot.

2b) 2♥. With 8 HCPs, and three-card support, raise partner's overcall to the two level.

2c) 3♥. A jump raise of partner's overcall is similar to a jump raise of partner's opening bid. It shows an invitational hand of about 11–12 points.

2d) 4♥. In addition to the 9 HCPs, you can count 3 dummy points for the singleton spade and 1 dummy point for the doubleton diamond. That's enough to take partner to the game level.

2e) 1NT. With 9 HCPs, but no support for partner's suit, and no suit of your own to show at the one level, respond 1NT.

You don't have enough strength to bid 2♣, a new suit at the two level.

2f) 1♠. With only two cards in partner's suit, bid your own suit. Most partnerships treat this as a forcing bid, and the overcaller will bid again. You'll then be in a better position to decide where the contract belongs.

3a) **Pass**. With only 4 HCPs, and a balanced hand, it appears that the best spot is a partscore in notrump, and you're already there.

3b) 2♠. Partner is showing a balanced hand, and should have at least two spades, giving the partnership an eight-card fit. Your response of 2♠ to partner's 1NT overcall is a sign-off bid. This isn't the same as a new suit in response to partner's bid of one-of-a-suit.

3c) **3NT**. You have a balanced hand with 10 HCPs plus 1 point for the five-card club suit. Take partner to the game level.

The Takeout Double

Don't be afraid to make a bid or a play. Remember: "A life spent making mistakes is not only more honorable but more useful than a life spent doing nothing."

— GEORGE BERNARD SHAW

Everyone loves a bargain, and the takeout double is like a two-for-one or three-for-one sale. It's an irresistible bid! To make good use of this bid, the partnership needs to work closely together. Let's see how you go about this.

The Takeout Double

Suppose the opponent on your right opens the bidding 1♥, and this is your hand:

♠ K J 7 2
♥ 4
♦ A J 7 3
♣ K Q 6 2

You were planning to open the bidding 1♦ for your side, but it's too late for that now. With the values for an opening bid, you would still like to compete for the contract. If you pass, you may end up defending with hearts as the trump suit. You'd like any suit other than hearts to be trump, preferably the suit in which partner has the most cards. With no good five-card or longer suit of your own to overcall, it would work out well if you could leave the choice of the trump suit to partner.

You can send this message to partner by saying "double" after your opponent's 1♥ bid. This is a *takeout double*, since it's a request to partner to take the double out and pick one of the *unbid* suits, a suit that hasn't been bid by the opponents. For example, the auction might proceed in this manner:

RHO	YOU	LHO	PARTNER
1♥	Double	Pass	1♠
	(*Pick a suit other than hearts*)		(*I like spades*)

The partnership works together to compete for the contract. Spades is selected as the trump suit. You promise the strength equivalent to an opening bid or better; partner picks the suit.

Support, Support, Support

One of the requirements for making a takeout double is to have support for whichever suit partner chooses. After all, you're asking partner to pick a suit. You don't want to end up playing in a contract where the opponents have more trumps than your side. It would be nice if you could always have at least four cards in whichever suit partner chooses. In practice, you may have less support for one of the possible suits, but you don't want to stray too far from the ideal unless you have extra strength.

With a choice, partner will generally prefer to bid a major suit rather than a minor suit. Major suit contracts are worth more than minor suit contracts. When making a takeout double, therefore, you should usually have four-card support for any major suit that partner might bid.

For example, consider each of these hands after the bidding is opened 1♦ on your right.

♠ Q 10 8 5
♥ A J 10 7
♦ 5
♣ A Q 6 3

This is the ideal pattern for a takeout double. You have shortness in the opponent's suit, and four-card support for each of the "unbid" suits.

♠ A Q J 5
♥ J 9 6 4
♦ 9 4
♣ A Q 6

This still qualifies for a takeout double because you have four-card support for hearts and spades, and reasonable three-card support if partner chooses clubs.

♠ 8 3
♥ K Q 8 5
♦ K 9 4 2
♣ A 7 5

This hand isn't suitable for a takeout double of 1♦. Although you have support for hearts, you don't have support if partner chooses spades, and your support isn't that good if partner picks clubs.

♠ K Q 9 4
♥ A K 10 7
♦ 5 4 2
♣ K Q

Although you don't have very good support for clubs, this hand should probably make a takeout double over the opponent's 1♦ bid. Hopefully, partner will bid hearts or spades, and everything will be fine. If partner bids clubs, you'll have to hope that your extra strength will make up for the poor support in that suit. A takeout double is preferable to an overcall of 1NT with this hand, since you don't have any strength in the opponent's suit.

♠ A K 9 8 4
♥ K 10 3
♦ 6 4
♣ Q 10 8

On this hand, you have a definite preference for the spade suit. You should overcall 1♠. Don't make a takeout double asking partner to choose the suit. You already know the suit you would like to suggest as trumps. I often tell my students, "If you know the answer, don't ask the question."

The Doubler's Dummy Points

To make a takeout double you need about the same values required for opening the bidding. If you ask partner to pick the suit, and your side ends up playing the contract, your hand will go down on the table as the dummy. Evaluate your hand using dummy points. For example, suppose the bidding is opened 1♠ on your right.

♠ 5
♥ K J 10 8
♦ A 10 9 6
♣ K 9 7 5

If you double, and partner bids clubs, diamonds, or hearts, and your side buys the contract, you'll be the dummy. It's as though partner bid the suit, and you're valuing your hand in support of partner's suit. You have only 11 HCPs, but you can count 3 dummy points for the singleton spade, bringing you to a total of 14 points. That's enough to make a takeout double.

♠ –
♥ A J 10 8
♦ 10 8 7 5 2
♣ K 9 8 4

There are only 8 HCPs, but your spade void can be counted as 5 dummy points. That gives you 13 points, enough for a takeout double. You expect to play this hand in a suit contract other than spades, with partner as declarer.

♠ 8 6
♥ Q J 7 2
♦ K 10 9
♣ A Q 8 7

You have 12 HCPs, and can count 1 dummy point for the doubleton spade. That's just enough for a takeout double. The further your hand is from the ideal shape for a takeout double, the more strength you need to compensate.

Double Trouble

Since a double is sometimes used as a *penalty double*, and sometimes as a takeout double, both partners need to understand which type of double is being made. To double loudly for penalties and softly for takeout isn't part of the game. Instead, you must rely on the logic of the situation.

Use the following guidelines:

- A double of an opponent's partscore contract is for takeout if your partner hasn't previously made a bid.
- A double is for penalty if either you or partner has already bid or the opponents are in a game level contract.

Some partnerships have more explicit agreements, but this understanding is sufficient for most partnerships. For example, suppose the auction starts like this:

LHO	PARTNER	RHO	YOU
1♠	Double	Pass	?

Partner's double is for takeout. 1♠ is a partscore contract, and this is partner's first opportunity to bid.

LHO	PARTNER	RHO	YOU
1♠	Pass	2♦	Double

Your double is for takeout. The opponents are still at the partscore level, and your partner hasn't made a bid. In this situation, your double would be asking partner to choose between hearts and clubs, the two unbid suits.

LHO	PARTNER	RHO	YOU
Pass	1♥	2♣	Double

This is a penalty double. Although your right-hand opponent's bid is still at the partscore level, your partner has already bid. There's no need to ask for partner's best suit. Some partnerships have special agreements about doubles in this type of sequence which are referred to as *negative doubles*. The standard agreement is that the double is for penalties.

LHO	PARTNER	RHO	YOU
1♠	Pass	3♠	Pass
4♠	Double		

Partner's double is for penalty, since the opponents are at the game level.

Doubling 1NT Opening Bids

There's one common exception to the guidelines. A double of an opponent's 1NT opening bid is usually treated as a penalty double. For example:

LHO	PARTNER	RHO	YOU
1NT	Double		

With only 13 cards, it's impossible for partner to have four-card support for all four unbid suits, so this double is more useful as a penalty double than as a takeout double. If an opponent opens the bidding with 1NT to show 16–18 points, it's rare that your side will want to come into the auction unless you have a good suit to overcall. You're generally better off to stay out of the auction.

Responding to a Takeout Double

Partner's takeout double shows the values for an opening bid, and asks you to pick a suit. Equipped with this knowledge, let's see how you go about responding to partner's request.

Getting the Message

A takeout double is forcing. You're being asked to bid, and aren't expected to pass. It's like a forcing bid. Suppose you have a hand like this:

♠ J 10 8 6
♥ 8 6 5
♦ 10 8 4 3
♣ 9 6

You're probably thinking that you won't be an active participant in the auction, even if partner opens the bidding. Suppose, however, the auction starts in this manner:

LHO	PARTNER	RHO	YOU
1♥	Double	Pass	?

Partner is asking you to bid. If you choose to pass, your left-hand opponent can pass, and the contract will be 1♥ doubled. If the opponents take seven or more tricks with hearts as trumps, they'll receive a bonus for making a doubled contract. Partner has asked you to pick anything except hearts as the trump suit. You should respect partner's request by bidding 1♠ with this hand, even though you have only 1 point.

Two Exceptions

Only if you have a lot of length and strength in the opponent's suit should you consider passing partner's takeout double. For example, you might pass in the above auction if this were your hand:

♠ 5 2
♥ K Q 10 9 8 7
♦ A 4
♣ 10 8 4

With this hand it looks as though hearts may be the best trump suit for your side, even if partner doesn't have any. This is the exception rather than the rule. In general, don't convert partner's takeout double into a penalty double by passing.

There's another situation that gives you a chance to pass partner's takeout double. If your right-hand opponent makes a bid, you no longer have to bid. For example:

LHO	PARTNER	RHO	YOU
1♥	Double	2♥	?

In this situation, you can pass if you don't have a good hand. Once the opponents bid, the effect of the double is "turned off." The opponents are in a partscore contract of 2♥, and you can pass. The opponent's bid doesn't prevent you from bidding if you have something to say—after all, partner does want to compete in the auction—but it does remove your obligation to bid.

Responding with 0–10 Points

With about 0–10 points, you comply with partner's request by bidding your best suit at the cheapest available level. Yes, with zero points, you're expected to bid! The takeout double shows the values for an opening bid—about 13 points—and unless partner has something extra, the partnership is looking for the best partscore.

With a choice of suits, the guidelines are familiar: bid your longest suit; bid the higher-ranking of two five-card suits; bid four-card suits up the line. One small exception is that you should prefer bidding a major suit rather than a minor suit. It's easier to compete in a major suit without increasing the level of bidding, and if there's enough combined strength for game, it requires less to make game in a major suit than in a minor suit.

Let's look at some examples when the bidding starts off:

LHO	PARTNER	RHO	YOU
1♦	Double	Pass	?

♠ 10 7 6 4 2
♥ 10 8 5
♦ 9 6 3
♣ 8 4

1♠. Since your right-hand opponent didn't bid, you must say something. Even though you have no high cards and can count only 1 point for the five-card suit, bid your longest suit at the cheapest available level. Partner has promised support for the suit that you choose.

♠ 10 6
♥ J 10 7 6
♦ 9 8 5
♣ A Q 6 2

1♥. Although your clubs are better than your hearts, it's better to show the major suit. You can do so at a lower level, and major suit contracts are worth more than minor suit contracts.

♠ Q 4
♥ 9 6 3
♦ 10 8 2
♣ Q J 8 6 4

2♣. Bid your longest suit at the cheapest available level. Although you're bidding a new suit at the two level, you don't need 11 or more points when responding to a takeout double. Partner has asked you to bid, and the situation is more comparable to raising partner's suit than to introducing a new suit of your own.

♠ 9 7 2   1NT. With no four-card suit to bid, and with
♥ Q 8 6   most of your strength in the opponent's suit,
♦ A J 9 8   a response of 1NT is your best choice. Part-
♣ Q 10 4   ner is unlikely to have many cards in the
                      opponent's suit when making a takeout
double. You should have some length and strength in the suit before considering bidding notrump.

There's a big difference between responding to a takeout double and responding to an opening bid of one-of-a suit. A new suit by responder is not forcing in this situation. This makes sense, since partner has forced you to bid a suit and you may have to bid with only one or two points.

Responding with 11–12 Points

When you hold 11 or 12 points, you want to make an invitational bid. You do this by jumping in your suit. Partner can turn down your invitation with only 13 or 14 points, but can carry on to game with a little extra.

This is similar to a limit raise, showing 11–12 points, and support for partner's suit. For example, suppose the bidding starts this way:

LHO	PARTNER	RHO	YOU
1♥	Double	Pass	?

♠ A Q 7 4   2♣. You would respond 1♠ with a hand in
♥ 6 3   the 0–10 point range. Here you have 11 HCPs,
♦ K J 8 6   and the partnership is close to the combined
♣ J 9 3   strength needed for a game contract. By jump-
                      ing a level of the bidding in response to
partner's takeout double, you send an invitational message. Partner can pass with the minimum values for a takeout double or bid on to game with a little extra.

♠ K 4
♥ J 9 2
♦ A Q 10 8 6 3
♣ 6 4

3♦. With 10 HCPs, and a six-card suit, make an invitational bid by jumping a level. Respond 3♦ rather than 2♦. You should be safe at the three level, since partner is showing an opening bid with support for the suit you choose. If partner has extra strength, a game contract is in sight.

♠ J 9 7
♥ A Q 10 4
♦ K Q 6
♣ 7 6 5

2NT. With no suit to show, and with lots of strength in the opponent's suit, make an invitational bid by jumping to 2NT to show your 12 HCPs. Partner should get the message. This is stronger than 1NT, but not as strong as bidding 3NT.

Responding with 13 or More Points

Once you hold 13 or more points, and partner makes a takeout double also showing the values for an opening bid, the partnership should end up in a game level contract. Usually, you'll be able to bid right to the appropriate contract. For example:

LHO	PARTNER	RHO	YOU
1♣	Double	Pass	?

♠ A 8 3
♥ K Q 7 6 5
♦ J 7 6
♣ Q J

4♥. Bid what you think you can make. Partner has the values for an opening bid with support for your heart suit. That's enough information to tell you what to do.

♠ A J 9 7
♥ 4 2
♦ A 7 5
♣ K J 6 3

4♠. It's possible that partner has only three-card support for spades, but partner will usually have four-card support for an unbid major suit. Game in spades looks like the correct spot for the partnership.

♠ Q 8
♥ J 7 5
♦ K Q 9 3 2
♣ A Q 10

3NT. You might consider bidding 5♦ with this hand, but it should be easier to take nine tricks in notrump than eleven tricks with diamonds as trump, especially when so much of your strength is in clubs.

Although, as responder, you'll usually know where to place the contract, there are times when you might want to make a forcing bid to get further information from partner. Since partner is asking you to pick any suit other than the one bid by the opponents, bidding the opponents' suit simply carries a forcing message back to the takeout doubler. For example, suppose your left-hand opponent bids 1♣, your partner doubles, and you hold this hand:

YOU
♠ A 10 9 4
♥ A J 6 4
♦ 10 8 3
♣ A 7

You want to be in game opposite partner's takeout double, but it isn't clear whether 4♥ or 4♠ would be best. You could pick one of the suits, and bid game, but it wouldn't hurt to get some further information from partner. Partner might, for example, have made a takeout double with this hand:

PARTNER
♠ K Q 8 5
♥ Q 7 3
♦ A Q 7 2
♣ 9 4

If you jump to 4♥, you won't end up in the best contract. Instead of guessing, you could make use of the cue bid. The auction might proceed in this manner:

LHO	PARTNER	RHO	YOU
1♣	Double	Pass	2♣
Pass	2♦	Pass	2♠
Pass	3♠	Pass	4♠
Pass	Pass	Pass	

With the help of the cue bid, you find your eight-card spade fit, and end up in the best contract. There are different styles of responses that the partnership can adopt through utilizing cue bids. You don't have to adopt them in your partnership to get where you're going—but you'll probably run into them sooner or later.

The Takeout Doubler's Next Call

If you make a takeout double, it's a forcing bid. You asked partner to bid even with very few points. Unless you have some extra strength or partner shows something extra by jumping or cue bidding, you've already done your share of competing.

With a Minimum-Strength Hand

With a hand in the 13–16 point range, you have the minimum strength for a takeout double. If partner responds at the cheapest available level, showing 0–10 points, you should pass when the bidding comes around to you. Partner could have no points at all, and you may already be way too high!

If partner jumps a level to show 11–12 points, you would still pass with only 13 or 14 points, rejecting partner's invitation. With 15 or 16 points, you can accept, and continue on to game.

If partner jumps right to game, you should accept partner's decision. You've already described your hand. Only if partner cue bids the opponents' suit are you forced to make another bid to further describe your hand.

Suppose you make a takeout double of an opponent's 1♦ opening bid with this hand:

♠ K J 8 5
♥ A J 7 6
♦ 10 3
♣ K J 6

If partner responds 1♥ or 1♠, showing 0–10 points, you should pass—and hope partner can make the contract. Even if partner makes an invitational bid by jumping to 2♥ or 3♣, for example, you should pass. You have nothing extra. You also have nothing more to say if partner bids a game contract such as 3NT or 4♠. Only if partner bids 2♦, cue bidding the opponent's suit, must you say something. You would bid 2♥, starting to show your suits "up the line." Partner is probably trying to find the best fit.

With a Medium-Strength Hand

When you make a takeout double with 17 or 18 points, a medium-strength hand, the partnership might still belong in game, even if partner responds at the cheapest level showing 0–10 points. You must proceed cautiously, however, since partner could have nothing.

If partner makes an invitational bid by jumping a level, you have more than enough to accept the invitation, and continue on to game. If partner bids to a game level contract, you should accept the decision. If partner wants more information from you before deciding on the contract, partner can start with a cue bid of the opponents' suit.

For example, suppose the bidding is opened 1♥ on your right, and you make a takeout double with this hand:

♠ A Q 10 4
♥ 6
♦ A Q J 5
♣ Q 10 7 3

You have 15 HCPs, and can count 3 dummy points for the singleton heart, giving you a total of 18 points. If partner responds 1♠, you should raise to 2♠, showing your extra strength. If partner has very little, you'll be more than high enough. With the top of the 0–10 point range, however, partner can now bid again, and the partnership will reach a game contract.

If partner were to make an invitational response, such as 2♠ or 3♣, jumping a level to show 11–12 points, you would carry on to game with this hand. If partner simply jumps to a game contract, such as 4♠, you would accept the decision, and pass.

With a Maximum-Strength Hand

With a maximum-strength hand of 19 or more points, proceed cautiously if partner shows a hand in the 0–10 point range. The more you have, the less partner is likely to have. You'll certainly get to game, and may even consider a slam contract, if partner makes an invitational or stronger response.

Suppose you make a takeout double of an opponent's 1♣ opening bid with this hand:

$$♠ \; A \, Q \, 8 \, 7$$
$$♥ \; A \, Q \, J \, 6$$
$$♦ \; K \, Q \, J$$
$$♣ \; J \, 3$$

A nice hand—20 HCPs! If partner were to respond 1♥, you might feel that the partnership belongs in a game contract. Partner, however, could have no points at all. Your takeout double was forcing, asking partner to bid a suit. Most of the remaining high cards are probably with the opening bidder. Instead of taking partner to the game level, you should raise to 3♥ with this hand. You're sending the message to partner to please carry on to game with a little something, but you're still allowing the partnership to stop in partscore.

If partner were to respond 2♥, showing an invitational hand of about 11–12 points, you would definitely get to game with this hand, and would probably consider bidding a slam. We'll leave the discussion of slam bidding for a later chapter. It's not too often that your side will get to a slam contract after the opponents have opened the bidding!

A Final Point

In the chapter on overcalls, it was mentioned that some partnerships prefer to put an upper limit of about 16 points on the range for a simple overcall. This style requires that you start with a takeout double when holding a hand of 17 or more points. For example:

♠ A 7
♥ A K J 9 7 4
♦ 8 6
♣ K J 3

If the opponents open the bidding 1♦, you would double with this hand rather than overcalling 1♥. Partner will respond by bidding a suit, under the assumption that you have a normal takeout double. Now you can bid your own suit or raise if partner responds 1♥.

This sequence of bids—doubling then bidding your suit—shows a hand too strong for an overcall. This falls in line with the earlier discussion about bidding again after making a takeout double only when you have a hand of 17 or more points.

Be sure you have a medium-strength hand or better when using the takeout double in this manner. Partner might jump to 2♠, or 4♠, expecting you to have support for the suit. With a very strong hand you can afford to make a takeout double without support for the unbid suits. The more strength you have, the less likely it is that partner will make a jump response, leaving you without enough room to show your suit. If partner does jump to a game contract, your extra strength should make up for the lack of trump support.

Summary

When the opponents open the bidding in a suit, you can compete for the contract by making a takeout double showing:

- Support for the other (unbid) suits.
- 13 or more points (counting dummy points).

You can distinguish a takeout double from a penalty double using the following criteria:

- A double of an opponent's partscore contract is for takeout if your partner has not previously made a bid. The only exception is an immediate double of an opening 1NT bid.
- A double is for penalty if either you or partner has already bid or the opponents are in a game level contract.

If partner makes a takeout double, use the following guidelines when making a response:

0–10 points	• Bid your longest suit at the cheapest available level.
11–12 points	• Bid your longest suit, jumping a level.
13 or more points	• Bid to a game contract.

With a choice of suits, prefer bidding a major suit to a minor suit. Without a good suit to bid, but with strength in the opponents' suit, bid notrump.

After you've made a takeout double, and partner makes a minimum response, you should pass unless you have a medium- or maximum- strength hand. If reponder shows 11 or 12 points, bid again if you think the partnership has enough for a game contract.

Exercises

1. The bidding is opened 1♦ on your right. What would you do with each of the following hands?

a) ♠ A J 8 6
♥ K 10 6 4
♦ 3
♣ K Q 9 2

b) ♠ J 9 7 4
♥ K 9 6 2
♦ J 7
♣ A 10 3

c) ♠ A 10 8 5
♥ J 10 7 4
♦ –
♣ K J 9 8 3

d) ♠ 8 4 2
♥ A 10 3
♦ A K J 8 6
♣ J 2

e) ♠ K 9 2
♥ A J 10 8 5
♦ A 6 4
♣ 9 2

f) ♠ K 10 5
♥ K J 8
♦ K J 10
♣ A Q 8 4

2. Is partner's double for takeout or penalty in the following auctions?

a)

LHO	PARTNER	RHO	YOU
		Pass	Pass
1♣	Double		

b)

LHO	PARTNER	RHO	YOU
1NT	Double		

c)

LHO	PARTNER	RHO	YOU
		1♠	Pass
4♠	Double		

d)

LHO	PARTNER	RHO	YOU
	Pass	1♦	Pass
2♦	Double		

3. What would you respond to partner's takeout double with each of the following hands after the auction starts:

LHO	PARTNER	RHO	YOU
1♥	Double	Pass	?

a) ♠ 5 3
    ♥ J 4
    ♦ J 8 7 6 2
    ♣ 10 8 4 3

b) ♠ Q 10 8 3
    ♥ K 5
    ♦ A 10 6 2
    ♣ 10 8 4

c) ♠ K J 9 5
    ♥ 6 3
    ♦ A J 8 7
    ♣ Q 9 4

d) ♠ Q 3
    ♥ 8 7 5
    ♦ A 2
    ♣ K J 10 8 5 3

e) ♠ J 10 8 7 3
    ♥ 5 2
    ♦ A K 8 6
    ♣ K J

f) ♠ J 8 3
    ♥ K Q 10 3
    ♦ J 9 7
    ♣ Q 8 6

Answers to Exercises

1a) **Double**. With 13 HCPs, and support for all the unbid suits, this is a perfect hand for a takeout double.

1b) **Pass**. Although there's support for the unbid suits, there isn't enough strength in this hand to make a takeout double.

1c) **Double**. Although there are only 9 HCPs, you can add 5 dummy points for the diamond void, giving this hand the values for a takeout double.

1d) **Pass**. Partner would interpret a double for takeout, and you don't have support for the unbid suits. You shouldn't overcall in the same suit bid by the opponents. Your best choice is to pass and see what happens.

1e) **1♥**. You don't have support for clubs, and have only three-card support for spades. The hand is more suitable for a simple overcall, showing your heart suit.

1f) **1NT**. With a balanced hand, 17 HCPs, and strength in the opponent's suit, make the natural overcall of 1NT. This is more descriptive than making a takeout double with this hand.

2a) **Takeout**. This is partner's first opportunity to bid. The opponents are at the partscore level, and you have not bid.

2b) **Penalty**. A direct double of a 1NT opening bid is for penalty, rather than takeout.

2c) **Penalty**. The opponents are at the game level.

2d) **Takeout**. Although partner didn't open the bidding, this is partner's first opportunity to double. The opponents are at the partscore level and you haven't bid.

3a) **2♦**. You shouldn't pass partner's takeout double, even though you don't have a very good hand. Instead, bid your longest suit at the cheapest available level.

3b) **1♠**. With 9 HCPs you are near the top of the range for a response at the cheapest available level. With a choice of four-card suits, prefer to show the major suit.

3c) **2♠**. With 11 HCPs, show the strength of your hand by jumping a level. This is an invitational response. Partner can pass with a minimal values for the takeout double. Otherwise, partner will continue on to game.

3d) **3♣.** There are 10 HCPs plus 2 points for the six-card suit. By jumping a level, rather than responding 2♣, you show an invitational hand of about 11–12 points.

3e) **4♠.** You have 12 HCPs plus 1 for the five-card spade suit. Bid game in your suit. Partner's takeout double has shown support for whichever suit you bid.

3f) **1NT.** With 9 HCPs, no good suit to show, and most of your strength in the opponent's suit, respond in notrump.

Competitive Bidding

"And when the last Great Scorer cometh
To Write against your name,
He'll ask not if you won or lost
But how you played the game."

— ALBERT EDYE

There are auctions that are quite lively, and every player is bidding. At times you want to check the backs of the cards to make certain only one deck is being used. Just as you have to deal with interruptions while you're working or having a conversation, you have to learn to handle the opponents' interference during the auction. It isn't that difficult—most of the time you can ignore them!

When an Opponent Overcalls

If an opponent makes an overcall when your side has opened the bidding, it takes up some of the bidding room. Sometimes this will affect your choice of bid; other times it won't. Let's see how you might handle various hands as responder when the auction starts in this manner:

LHO	PARTNER	RHO	YOU
	1♣	1♥	?

♠ A J 8 7 5
♥ 8 4
♦ K 9 3
♣ 8 4 2

1♠. No problem here. You were intending to respond 1♠, and your right-hand opponent's overcall doesn't prevent you from continuing with your original plan.

♠ K J 5 2
♥ Q 10 4
♦ K Q 6 3
♣ 7 4

1♠. You were originally going to respond 1♦, starting to bid your four-card suits "up the line." There's no room to do that now, but you can still show your four-card spade suit at the one level.

♠ Q 4
♥ 7 4 2
♦ A Q J 10 5
♣ K 8 4

2♦. Without interference, you would have responded 1♦, bidding your long suit. You can still show your diamond suit, but it will have to be at the two level. You need about 11 or more points to respond in a new suit at the two level. You have 12 HCPs plus 1 for the fifth diamond on this hand.

♠ 9 7 4
♥ K 10 8 5
♦ A 9 3
♣ Q 6 2

1NT. You would have responded 1♥ if your opponent hadn't bid. You can substitute a 1NT response. You have a hand in the 6–10 point range, but no four-card or longer suit that can be shown at the one level. To suggest notrump as a contract, you should have some strength in the opponent's suit, which you do in this case.

♠ J 4
♥ 8 7 4
♦ K 9 6 2
♣ A 10 8 3

2♣. This is awkward. Without the interference, you could have responded 1♦. You would like to have five-card support to raise opener's minor suit, but sometimes you have to make do with what you're dealt.

♠ 7 5
♥ A Q J 9 8 5
♦ K 7 2
♣ 8 5

Double. This is a penalty double, not a take-out double, because partner has already made a bid. You're voicing your opinion that the opponents can't take seven tricks with hearts as trump, especially since your partner has the values for an opening bid. This may not end the auction, but it's the best way to get the message across to partner that you have great length and strength in the heart suit. It will be interesting to see what happens next!

♠ K 3 2
♥ 10 7
♦ Q 10 9 7 5 3
♣ J 8

Pass. The opponent's bid has taken away your natural response of 1♦. You don't have enough strength to respond 2♦, a new suit at the two level. The alternative of bidding 1NT is unattractive with no length or strength in the opponent's suit.

There's nothing wrong with passing when you have no good alternative. The reason you usually respond with 6 or more points is in case partner has a maximum-strength hand. You don't want to miss a game contract. In this situation partner will get another opportunity to bid, and can show a strong hand. If you then show your diamond suit, partner will be aware that you have less than 11 points, since you didn't bid immediately over the opponent's overcall.

Passing as responder with a hand in the 6–10 point range is a new option when your opponent enters the bidding.

When an Opponent Doubles

The opponent's double doesn't use up any of your bidding room, so you can continue to comfortably exchange information. For example, suppose the auction starts this way:

LHO	PARTNER	RHO	YOU
	1♦	Double	?

♠ 9 6
♥ A Q J 7 5
♦ Q 4 2
♣ 10 8 5

1♥. This is what you were planning to respond. Don't let the opponents stop you.

♠ K 8 3
♥ 9 4
♦ Q J 8 6 2
♣ Q 6 2

2♦. Raise partner's suit, as you would have done without the double. The opponent's double is for takeout, not for penalty. If you pass, your left-hand opponent will bid. By bidding first, you'll make it more difficult for the opponents to compete for the contract.

♠ J 8 5
♥ Q 9 3
♦ 10 4
♣ J 8 7 5 2

Pass. You weren't planning to bid with this hand. Nothing has changed.

Redouble—Toil and Trouble

When the opponents double your partner's bid they create a new option for you, the *redouble*. The original intent of the redouble was similar to that of the double: to further increase the score if the contract is made or defeated. Like the double, however, the redouble has been put to additional use.

Using the redouble correctly when an opponent doubles your partner's opening bid of one-of-a-suit takes some practice. Let's take a look at how it can be used.

The guideline for using the redouble in this situation is straightforward enough:

* Redouble with 10 or more HCPs.

The message you're sending partner is: "This is our hand; we have the balance of strength." The consequence of sending this message isn't so clear. It changes the meaning of your other responses, and you must be prepared to follow up with a suitable rebid.

Since a redouble shows any hand with 10 or more HCPs, the inference is that any other response you make shows less than 10 HCPs. This can prove useful in a competitive situation, and is the reason many players like to make use of the redouble. For example, suppose the bidding starts like this:

LHO	PARTNER	RHO	YOU
	1♥	Double	?

♠ Q J 10 8 6
♥ 7 5
♦ K 9 4 2
♣ 8 5

1♠. This appears to be the same response you would make without the double, but there's a subtle difference. A new suit at the one level by responder normally shows 6 or more points, an unlimited bid. Here, partner can infer that you have at most 10 HCPs. With more, you would have started with a redouble.

♠ 8 5
♥ 9 4
♦ Q J 10 9 7 6
♣ K 8 2

2♦. You wouldn't be able to show your diamond suit with this hand in response to partner's opening bid of 1♥. A new suit at the two level requires 11 or more points. Instead, you would respond 1NT. After the double, you have an opportunity to show your suit because only a redouble shows 10 or more HCPs.

♠ 5
♥ K J 8 4
♦ 6 4 2
♣ Q 9 8 6 5

3♥. Without the double, a jump raise of partner's suit to the three level would show about 11–12 points, assuming your partnership style is to use limit raises. After the double, you can jump to 3♥ to show good support for partner's suit, but not much strength, since you would redouble with 10 or more HCPs.

Jumping to 3♥ has the advantage of making it more difficult for the opponents to find their best contract when they hold the balance of strength. You could bid only 2♥ with this hand, but your left-hand opponent might have enough strength to bid 2♠ or 3♦. If you respond 3♥, your opponent might not be willing to compete with 3♠ or 4♦, and your side may win the auction.

This all makes sense, but both you and your partner now have two sets of responses to remember: those when there's no double, and those after an opponent's takeout double.

The other thing you must be prepared to do if you use the redouble is to follow up with the appropriate bid on the next round of the auction. You haven't described your hand when you redouble, other than to say that you have 10 or more HCPs. Whether your left-hand opponent bids or passes, partner is generally expected to pass and wait to see what you have to say next. For example, suppose the auction goes like this:

LHO	PARTNER	RHO	YOU
	1♥	Double	Redouble
1♠	Pass	Pass	?

♠ A Q J 8 6
♥ 7
♦ A 9 7 3
♣ 8 6 2

Double. This is one of the reasons you start with a redouble rather than responding 1♠ on this hand. You may get an opportunity to double the opponents in their contract, and, hopefully, collect a large penalty. Partner has cooperated by passing the auction back to you rather than bidding.

♠ A 5
♥ 9 2
♦ A K J 8 7 5
♣ J 6 2

2♦. You couldn't bid 2♦ right away over the takeout double because that would show fewer than 10 HCPs. Instead, you start with a redouble, and then bid your suit at the next opportunity.

♠ Q 8
♥ A 7 5
♦ K 9 6 4
♣ Q 10 8 3

2♥. You didn't support hearts right away because you have 11 HCPs. By redoubling first, and then showing your heart support, partner will have a description of your hand. Notice that you don't have to jump to 3♥ with this hand, since you've already promised at least 10 points by redoubling.

As you can see, there's a bit of toil and trouble in learning to use the redouble. Your partnership may prefer getting by without it.

Summary

When both sides are competing for the auction, you have to do the best that you can. Sometimes, the opponents' bids won't get in your way. At other times, you may have to find a different bid than the one you were originally planning to make. If you can't think of a good bid, try passing. In most competitive auctions you'll get another chance later if the contract belongs to your side.

You can use the redouble to show a hand of 10 or more HCPs when your partner's opening bid at the one level is doubled by an opponent, but only if both you and your partner have discussed how it works. Otherwise, ignore the opponent's double, and make your normal response.

Exercises

1. What would you respond with each of the following hands after the auction starts:

LHO	PARTNER	RHO	YOU
Pass	1♥	1♠	?

a) ♠ J 10 7 3
   ♥ J 5
   ♦ Q 9 6 2
   ♣ 8 7 4

b) ♠ 8 3
   ♥ A 5
   ♦ A K 10 6 2
   ♣ Q 9 7 5

c) ♠ 9 5
   ♥ Q 8 7
   ♦ K Q 8 7 3
   ♣ J 9 3

d) ♠ A J 3
   ♥ 7 6
   ♦ Q 9 6 2
   ♣ K 10 7 5

e) ♠ 8 6
   ♥ 5 2
   ♦ J 8 6
   ♣ K J 10 7 5 2

f) ♠ J 8 3
   ♥ K Q 10 3
   ♦ 9 7
   ♣ A J 8 6

2. Assuming your partnership makes use of the redouble, what would you respond with each of the following hands after the auction starts:

LHO	PARTNER	RHO	YOU
	1♦	Double	?

a) ♠ 9 4
   ♥ K J 10 8 5
   ♦ K 8
   ♣ J 7 6 4

b) ♠ K 10 5
   ♥ Q J 6
   ♦ 10 6
   ♣ K 9 8 7 5

c) ♠ Q 10 4
   ♥ 8 7
   ♦ 7 3
   ♣ A J 10 8 7 3

d) ♠ A K J 7
   ♥ K Q 9 4
   ♦ 2
   ♣ Q 8 6 4

e) ♠ A K J 8 6
   ♥ K 7 3
   ♦ 8 6
   ♣ J 10 5

f) ♠ 8 3
   ♥ 10
   ♦ A J 9 7 5
   ♣ K 7 6 5 2

Answers to Exercises

1a) **Pass**. You weren't going to bid before right-hand opponent intervened, and there's no reason to change your mind.

1b) **2♦**. This was your intended response to partner's 1♥ opening bid, since you have enough strength to bid a new suit at the two level. The 1♠ overcall hasn't interfered.

1c) **2♥**. You have support for partner's suit and a hand in the 6–10 point range. Don't let the opponent's overcall deter you from making your natural response.

1d) **1NT**. That's the response you would have made if your right-hand opponent had passed. With some strength in the opponent's spade suit, you can make the same bid, letting partner know you have a hand in the 6–10 point range.

1e) **Pass**. You have 5 HCPs and can add 2 points for the six-card suit. You were originally planning to respond 1NT, since you don't have enough strength to show your suit at the two level. That bid is unappealing now that your right-hand opponent has shown a good spade suit. With nothing much to say, pass for now. The auction isn't over and you'll get another chance to bid if partner shows a strong hand.

1f) **3♥**. You have 11 HCPs plus 1 dummy point for the doubleton diamond. You can make a limit raise to 3♥, showing 11–12 points, as if your opponent had never entered the auction.

2a) **1♥**. This is the response you would have made without the double. The double hasn't taken away any of your bidding room, so go ahead.

2b) **1NT**. You have 9 HCPs plus 1 for the five-card suit. Make your normal response of 1NT as though the double never occurred.

2c) **2♣**. You wouldn't be able to respond 2♣ if your opponent hadn't doubled because you have less than 11 points. You can afford to show your suit in this situation because you would have redoubled with 10 or more HCPs, so partner will not be expecting too much.

2d) **Redouble**. With 15 HCPs, you want to tell partner that the hand belongs to your side. When the opponents bid a suit, you should plan to double their contract for penalties. It's unlikely that they can take many tricks when you have this much strength, and partner has the values for an opening bid.

2e) **Redouble**. If you respond 1♠, partner will assume that you have less than 10 HCPs because you didn't redouble. With 12 HCPs, start by redoubling. If the opponents bid spades, you can double their contract. Otherwise, you can show your spades at your next turn, and partner will have a good description of your hand.

2f) **3♦**. Although you have only 8 HCPs, you can jump to 3♦ because partner won't expect much strength when you didn't redouble. You want to get your bid in early, before the opponents have room to find their best spot. Hopefully, your bid will keep them out of the remainder of the auction.

Part 6

OPENINGS
BEYOND
THE ONE LEVEL

Big Hands— and Big Bids

"Your temperament will be much more appealing if you're satisfied with the best result possible rather than the best possible result."

It's nice to have a partner, but sometimes you're dealt a hand like this:

YOU
♠ 6
♥ A K Q J 10 9
♦ A K
♣ A K 6 5

You can make a game contract all by yourself. Partner could hold
no points at all, but you would still take 10 tricks opposite a hand
like this:

PARTNER
♠ 9 4 3 2
♥ 7 4 2
♦ 8 6 5
♣ 10 4 3

Why not open the bidding 4♥ and be done with it? Let's take a
closer look.

Big Unbalanced Hands—Strong Two Bids

One reason that you don't want to open the above hand with a bid
of 4♥ is that your side may be able to get a slam bonus. Partner
could hold a hand like this:

PARTNER
♠ Q 10 3 2
♥ 7 4 2
♦ 8 6 5
♣ Q J 3

Now you can take 12 tricks: six heart tricks, two diamond tricks,
and four club tricks.

Furthermore, the best contract might not be with hearts as the
trump suit. Partner could have a hand like this:

PARTNER
♠ 5 4 3
♥ 2
♦ Q J 10 9 3 2
♣ 10 4 3

6♦ is a better contract than 6♥.

With big hands, you still need to explore for the best contract.
You don't want to open the bidding 1♥. Your partner would pass

with all of the above hands, and you would miss your game or slam contract. The solution is to open the bidding with a forcing bid— one that partner can't pass but that still leaves enough room in the auction to find the right contract.

The Strong Two-Bid

The standard way of showing a strong unbalanced hand is to open the bidding at the two level rather than the one level: 2♣, 2♦, 2♥, or 2♠. This *strong two-bid* is a special forcing bid asking partner to keep bidding until game is reached.

Once you've started with a strong two-bid, partner won't pass until you're at least at the game level. This gives both of you room to describe your hands, and find the best spot. Partner will also be aware that a slam contract is a possibility if there's a little extra strength between the two hands.

You need a good hand, generally 22 or more points, to demand that partner keep the bidding going until game is reached. For example:

♠ A K Q 6 ♥ A K J 8 7 ♦ 3 ♣ A Q 4	2♥. With 23 HCPs plus 1 for the five-card suit, open the bidding with a strong two-bid in your longest suit. With this hand it's difficult to say what the best contract will be without knowing something about partner's hand. The partner-

ship may belong in 4♥, 4♠, 3NT, or 6♣. You'll have room to investigate knowing the partnership is committed to at least the game level.

♠ 3 ♥ A 4 ♦ A K J 9 3 ♣ A K Q J 6	2♦. With a choice of two five-card suits, open the higher-ranking. You plan to show the clubs next. You have 22 HCPs plus 1 for each of the five-card suits.

♠ A K Q 7 4 ♥ K Q 8 ♦ A J 7 5 ♣ 2	1♠. This is a nice hand, but there are only 19 HCPs plus 1 for the fifth spade. This isn't enough to commit the partnership to the game level. Start at the one level. If partner doesn't have enough strength to make a re-

sponse, you'll be high enough. If partner does respond, you can
show your maximum-strength hand.

♠ A K Q 10 9 7 4   2♠. Sometimes you need to use a little judg-
♥ 7 4   ment. This hand is valued as 20 points—17
♦ A K J 10   HCPs plus 3 points for the seven-card suit. Yet
♣ –   you expect to take about ten tricks even if
                     partner has nothing: seven spade tricks, and
three diamond tricks. The 22 point requirement is a guideline. Some
20 point hands are better than others!

There are other ways to show strong hands. Strong two-bids, however, are easy to use, and they sound like what they are—a hand too
strong to open at the one level.

Responding to a Strong Two-Bid

You pick up a hand like this, and you hear your partner open the
bidding 2♥:

♠ 9 4 3 2
♥ 7 4 2
♦ 8 6 5
♣ 10 4 3

Does it look familiar? I'll bet you don't feel like saying anything
except "pass" with this hand. Partner's strong two-bid, however, is
forcing to game. Partner may have a hand like the one at the beginning of the chapter, and will be very sad if you pass.

You have to bid something to keep the auction going, and the
common agreement is this:

• A response of 2NT shows a poor hand of about 0–5 points.

This is sometimes called a *negative response*. It's an artificial, or
conventional, bid, since it has nothing to do with a desire to play in
notrump. It sends the message to partner that you don't have much
to contribute in the way of strength.

Anything else you bid shows about 6 or more points. With three or more cards you can support partner's suit. You can show a good suit of your own. With a balanced hand of about 6–10 points, you can jump to 3NT, since 2NT shows 0–5 points.

Let's try a few hands in response to an opening bid of 2♥ from partner.

♠ J 8 5
♥ 8 3
♦ Q 9 7 2
♣ 10 8 7 4

2NT. This is the negative response, telling partner you don't have much help to offer on this hand. If partner now rebids 3♥, you must bid again, since the partnership is committed to the game level. You would raise to 4♥.

♠ Q 10 8 7 5 2
♥ 8
♦ 7 5
♣ 9 6 4 3

2NT. The response of 2NT doesn't show a balanced hand. It sends the message to partner that you have a weak hand. When partner makes a rebid of 3♦ or 3♥, for example, you can now show your suit by bidding 3♠. Partner will not expect you to have too much because of your initial 2NT response.

♠ 7 4
♥ Q 8 5
♦ J 10 7 5
♣ K 9 8 2

3♥. Partner has an unbalanced hand with five or more hearts. Your three-card support and 6 HCPs are enough to raise. By agreeing on hearts right away, the partnership can now decide between stopping at the game level or going to the slam level.

♠ K Q 10 7 4
♥ 10 2
♦ Q J 6 3
♣ 9 3

2♠. Without support for partner's suit, but with a good suit of your own, and enough strength for a positive response, show your suit. The partnership is exploring for the best place to play the hand.

♠ K Q 5
♥ J 4
♦ J 10 7 5
♣ Q 10 8 3

3NT. With 9 HCPs, but only two cards in partner's suit, and no good suit of your own to show, bid 3NT. You shouldn't respond 2NT because that would show less than 6 points. Generally you need a good five-card suit to introduce it as an alternative to partner's trump suit.

♠ 7 4
♥ J 8 6 4
♦ Q 10 7 5
♣ 8 7 3

2NT or 4♥. This hand falls in the negative response category, and you could start with a response of 2NT, planning to show the support for partner's suit at your next turn. Some partnerships prefer to use an immediate jump to game to show this type of hand—good trump support but nothing much else, no aces, kings, singletons, or voids in the other suits.

The Rest of the Auction

After the initial response, opener continues to describe the hand. The partnership is under no pressure to jump to the game level. Here are some typical bidding conversations when there is a big hand involved.

OPENER	RESPONDER
♠ A K Q 10 8 7 4	♠ 9 6
♥ 4	♥ J 8 5 3
♦ A K J	♦ 10 7 6 4
♣ K 4	♣ Q 8 2

2♠	*I have a really good hand with a spade suit.*	2NT	*I don't have much.*
3♠	*I think spades should be the trump suit.*	4♠	*Okay.*
Pass	*I guess we've arrived.*		

	OPENER		RESPONDER
	♠ A 7 3		♠ Q 10 8 6 4 2
	♥ A K J 10 8		♥ 3
	♦ 5		♦ J 9 3
	♣ A K Q 6		♣ 8 5 2

2♥	*I have a strong hand with hearts.*	2NT	*I don't have a good hand . . .*
3♣	*I've also got a nice club suit.*	3♠	*. . . but I do have a long spade suit.*
4♠	*Sounds good to me.*	Pass	*How did I end up playing this hand!*

	OPENER		RESPONDER
	♠ A K Q 8 7 5		♠ 2
	♥ –		♥ K 6 2
	♦ A K Q 7 5		♦ J 10 8 3
	♣ Q 6		♣ K J 10 7 5

2♠	*Don't pass.*	3♣	*I've got enough to say something positive.*
3♦	*How about diamonds?*	4♦	*I prefer diamonds to spades.*
6♦	*That's what I needed to hear.*	Pass	*This should be fun.*

There are other ways to bid to slam—but you get the idea.

Small, Medium, and Large Balanced Hands

You open 2NT to show a balanced hand with 22–24 points, and 3NT to show a balanced hand with 25–27 points. If you hold more than 27 points, I hope I don't have to play against you very often!

This seems like a good time to consider how to describe a balanced hand of any strength:

0–12 points	Pass.
13–15 points	Open one-of-a-suit, planning to rebid notrump at the cheapest level at your next opportunity.
16–18 points	Open 1NT.
19–21 points	Open one-of-a-suit, planning to jump in notrump at your next opportunity.
22–24 points	Open 2NT.
25–27 points	Open 3NT.

Responding to 2NT

An opening bid of 2NT, interestingly enough, isn't a forcing bid. Since opener has limited the hand to at most 24 points, responder can pass with a very weak hand, leaving the partnership to play in partscore. Otherwise, responder bids in a manner very similar to responding to 1NT, although there isn't enough room left to sign off in partscore in a suit. Use the following guidelines:

0–2 points	• Pass.
3–8 points	• Bid 4♥ or 4♠ with a six-card or longer suit.
	• Bid 3♥ or 3♠ (forcing) with a five-card suit.
	• Bid 3♣ (Stayman) with a four-card major suit.
	• Otherwise, bid 3NT.

The Stayman Convention is discussed separately in a later chapter. With 9 or more points, your target should be the slam level, and

there will be more discussion about that later on. For now, let's see
how you would handle the following hands after partner opens 2NT.

♠ 10 9 7 4   Pass. Your 1 point is unlikely to be enough
♥ 8 6 2   to help partner take nine tricks. This is the
♦ J 6 4   time to pass, and leave the partnership in
♣ 10 8 5   partscore.

♠ Q 10 8 6 4 2   4♠. You have 4 HCPs plus 2 for the six-card
♥ 4   spade suit. There should be enough com-
♦ 7 5   bined strength for a game contract. Partner's
♣ Q 8 6 3   balanced hand will contain at least two spades,
                    so there's an eight-card major suit fit.

♠ Q 5   3♥. With 5 HCPs plus 1 for the five-card
♥ K 10 8 6 4   suit, the partnership belongs in game. A re-
♦ 7 5   sponse of 3♥ is forcing. Opener will bid 3NT
♣ 10 8 6 3   holding only two hearts, but will continue on
                    to 4♥ with three-card or longer support.

♠ 7 4   3NT. With no major suit to show, raise part-
♥ 10 8 2   ner to game in notrump. The partnership has
♦ K 9 6 3   at least 26 combined points, and partner
♣ J 10 7 5   should have a chance at taking nine tricks.

Responding to 3NT

There's not much room to explore when partner opens the bidding
3NT. You're already in a game contract. Put the partnership in its
eight-card major suit fit by bidding 4♥ or 4♠ with a six-card or longer
suit. Otherwise, pass unless you're interested in getting to a slam
contract. Here are some examples of responding to partner's
3NT opening.

♠ J 8
♥ 7 4
♦ J 10 8 7 2
♣ 9 7 5 3

Pass. It's a good thing partner has 25–27 points. You aren't going to provide much help with this hand.

♠ 5
♥ 10 8 7 5 4 2
♦ 9 7 6 3
♣ 8 3

4♥. You have no high cards, but the partnership should still be playing in a major suit with an eight-card or longer fit.

♠ K 10 8
♥ J 9 4
♦ K J 8 6
♣ 10 7 2

6NT. Adding your 8 HCPs to partner's 25–27 points gives the partnership at least 33 combined points. That should be enough to go for the slam bonus, and try to take 12 tricks.

Going for the Slam Bonus

The basic criteria for bidding to the slam level is fairly straightforward:

- 33 or more combined points for a small slam contract.
- 37 or more combined points for a grand slam contract.

The challenge comes in finding out whether or not you have the combined strength, and in deciding where you want to play the hand, in a suit or in notrump.

Totaling Up

Adding up the points to determine whether there are enough for a slam is no different than adding them up to decide whether the partnership has the 26 combined points needed for a game contract. Once one partner limits the hand to a narrow range of points, the other partner should know whether or not the contract belongs in the slam zone. Listen to these auctions:

OPENER
♠ A K 10
♥ K J 8 7
♦ A 8 5
♣ Q 6 2

RESPONDER
♠ Q 9 3
♥ A Q 3
♦ K Q 2
♣ K J 8 5

1NT *I have a balanced hand with 16–18 points.*

6NT *We have at least 33 combined points and at most 35.*

Pass *You're the captain.*

OPENER
♠ K J 10 4
♥ A K J 7 4
♦ 8
♣ Q 9 5

RESPONDER
♠ A Q 7 6 3 2
♥ 3
♦ A 9
♣ A 6 3 2

1♥ *I have an opening bid with at least a five-card heart suit.*

1♠ *I'll bid a new suit at the one level (forcing) and see what partner says.*

3♠ *I have good support for your suit. With 14 HCPs plus 3 dummy points for the singleton, I have a medium-strength hand.*

6♠ *You have 17–18 points and I have 14 HCPs plus 2 for the six-card suit. We should have the 33 combined points we need for a slam contract.*

Pass *I guess we've arrived.*

OPENER	RESPONDER
♠ –	♠ A 9 7
♥ A K J 4	♥ Q 10 3
♦ A J 10 8 7 4	♦ K Q 9 6 3
♣ K Q J	♣ 3 2

	OPENER		RESPONDER
1♦	*I hope partner has enough to respond.*	3♦	*Five-card support and 11 HCPs, enough for a limit raise.*
6♦	*Opposite 11–12 points, I'll take my chances.*	Pass	*Good luck partner.*

There are other ways to bid to the slam level, but this is the basic idea when you know there's enough combined strength.

If you aren't sure that there's enough strength, you can invite partner to slam by bidding one level beyond game. For example:

OPENER	RESPONDER
♠ Q J 7 2	♠ K 9 6
♥ K Q 4	♥ A J 8
♦ K 9 6	♦ Q J 7
♣ A J 10	♣ K Q 8 6

	OPENER		RESPONDER
1NT	*Another one of those balanced hands with 16–18 points.*	4NT	*I have 16 HCPs. We have somewhere between 32 and 34 points.*
Pass	*Sorry partner. I'm at the bottom of my range.*		

OPENER	RESPONDER
♠ K 10	♠ A J
♥ K Q 6 4	♥ J 10 8 7 5 2
♦ K Q 8 7 5	♦ A J
♣ J 9	♣ A Q 8

1♦	*Longest suit first.*	1♥	*Let's try to find our fit.*
2♥	*I like your hearts, but I have only a minimum strength opening bid.*	5♥	*I've got 17 HCPs plus 2 for my long suit. We're close to the slam level. Anything extra partner?*
6♥	*Well, I'm at the top end of the range for a minimum-strength hand.*	Pass	*Hope I haven't overdone it!*

Again, there are fancier methods that can be employed when thinking of going to the slam level, but this should get the job done.

Finding the Fit

Find out whether you have a suitable trump fit before galloping off into the slam zone. There won't be room left to explore once you get there.

One nice thing about the slam level is that the minor suits become as important as the major suits. You have to take twelve tricks to make your slam whether you're in 6♥ or 6♦. You want to be in your best trump suit. Only when you don't have a good fit in a suit do you want to play slam in notrump.

If you think there's enough strength for a slam, but aren't sure about where to play the contract, make another forcing bid asking partner to further describe the hand. As a general guideline, **a bid of a new suit by responder is forcing**, except after a 1NT opening bid or rebid by opener.

Here are some examples of finding your fit before bidding a slam.

OPENER	RESPONDER
♠ K Q 7 2	♠ A 9 5
♥ A Q 8	♥ K J 10 7 3
♦ K 7	♦ A 8 5
♣ Q 9 7 3	♣ A 6

1NT	*I have a balanced hand with 16–18 points.*	3♥	*I have 16 HCPs plus 1 for the five-card suit. Enough for a slam, but we need to find a fit.*
4♥	*I have three-card support for your suit.*	6♥	*Good. Now that I know where we belong I can bid our slam.*
Pass	*That was a bit of a surprise.*		

OPENER	RESPONDER
♠ Q 10 8 3	♠ A K J 4
♥ K 7	♥ A Q 8 2
♦ A K 9 6	♦ 10 7
♣ J 5 4	♣ K Q 8

1♦	*I have a balanced hand, but not enough to open 1NT.*	1♥	*I'm pretty sure we belong at the slam level but we better find a fit first.*
1♠	*I don't have support for your hearts, but I will keep showing my suits up the line.*	6♠	*Aha! Now I've uncovered our eight-card major suit fit. With 19 HCPs and a doubleton, I think we should go for the slam bonus.*
Pass	*Well, I certainly have nothing more to say. How did we get so high?*		

Keeping Control

Once you've found your fit, and there appears to be enough combined strength for slam, there's one other consideration. In a small slam, you don't want the opponents taking the first two tricks. In a grand slam, you certainly don't want them taking the first trick with an ace before you get a chance to take your tricks.

To prevent the opponents from taking tricks right away, your side wants to hold most of the aces and kings. If you have all four aces, for example, the opponents can't take the first trick, and you'll have an opportunity to make your contract. If you're missing two aces, it doesn't matter how many tricks you can take when you gain the lead, the opponents can take the first two, defeating your slam contract.

Voids and singletons can act as aces and kings in a trump contract, preventing the opponents from taking their winners. These are all called *controls* because they control the first or second round of the suit.

Finding out about the controls held by your side is a challenge. Most of the time you can bid your slam, and trust that the necessary aces and kings will be there. Experienced partnerships sometimes show their controls by cue bidding them after a trump suit has been agreed. That's a little beyond the scope of this book. An alternative is to use an artificial, or conventional, method of asking partner about the number of aces and kings held. This is covered in Chapter 16.

For now, go for the big bonus when your side has the strength and the fit. The refinements can wait.

Summary

Use the following bids to show your really big hands:

2♣, 2♦, 2♥, 2♠   • 22 or more points and an unbalanced hand, forcing to game.

2NT   • 22–24 points and a balanced hand, invitational.

3NT   • 25–27 points and a balanced hand.

A strong two-bid (2♣, 2♦, 2♥, 2♠) is forcing to the game level, and responder bids as follows:

0–5 points   • Bid 2NT (artificial, negative response).

6 or more points • Support partner's suit.
    • Bid a new suit.
    • Bid 3NT.

Respond to an opening 2NT bid using these guidelines:

0–2 points   • Pass.

3–8 points   • Bid 4♥ or 4♠ with six-card or longer suit.
    • Bid 3♥ or 3♠ (forcing) with five-card suit.
    • Bid 3♣ (Stayman) with a four-card major suit. (See Chapter 16.)
    • Otherwise, bid 3NT.

After exploring for a trump fit, the partnership should consider bidding a slam contract with sufficient strength between the partnership hands:

Small Slam (six level)   • 33 or more combined points.

Grand Slam (seven level) • 37 or more combined points.

If you're unsure whether or not there's enough strength for a slam, you can send an invitation to partner by bidding beyond the game level. Partner can pass or accept with extra strength.

Exercises

1. What would be your opening bid with each of the following hands?

a) ♠ —
♥ A K J 10 7 5
♦ K J 4
♣ A K Q 4

b) ♠ K Q 10 5
♥ A J
♦ K J 9 4
♣ A K J

c) ♠ A K
♥ K Q 4
♦ A Q J 7 5
♣ A Q 4

d) ♠ K Q J 9 7
♥ 7 6
♦ A K 6 5
♣ K Q

e) ♠ A K Q 8 6
♥ 2
♦ A K Q J 5
♣ K 4

f) ♠ A K Q J 8 7
♥ 8
♦ 9 7
♣ A K Q 10

2. What would you respond with each of the following hands if your partner opened the bidding 2♥ (a strong two-bid)?

a) ♠ J 9 8 5 2
♥ 5 4
♦ Q 6 3
♣ 10 8 4

b) ♠ A 9 7 3
♥ K 8 5 2
♦ 10 4
♣ 9 6 2

c) ♠ 5 2
♥ 4
♦ J 9 8 6 4 3 2
♣ J 7 6

d) ♠ 8 7
♥ J 3
♦ Q 9 6 2
♣ A Q J 7 5

e) ♠ Q J 8
♥ 10 2
♦ Q J 7 5
♣ K 10 8 3

f) ♠ J 8 7
♥ J 9 8 6
♦ 10 8 7 5
♣ Q 4

3. What would you respond with each of these hands after partner opens the bidding 2NT?

a) ♠ K 8 3
   ♥ 5 4
   ♦ Q 9 6 4
   ♣ 8 7 4 2

b) ♠ K J 10
   ♥ K J 9
   ♦ Q J 7
   ♣ 9 8 6 2

c) ♠ Q J 9
   ♥ K 3
   ♦ 10 9 7 5
   ♣ K 9 6 3

4. What would you do next on each of these hands after the bidding starts:

LHO	PARTNER	RHO	YOU
Pass	1♣	Pass	1♠
Pass	4♠	Pass	?

a) ♠ Q 9 7 3
   ♥ 10 4 2
   ♦ J 5 3
   ♣ A 8 6

b) ♠ K J 10 8 7 6
   ♥ A 9 4 2
   ♦ K 6 2
   ♣ –

c) ♠ 10 9 7 5 3
   ♥ A 8 3
   ♦ A 10 5
   ♣ K 6

Answers to Exercises

1a) 2♥. 21 HCPs plus two points for the six-card suit is enough to start the auction off with a strong two-bid.

1b) 2NT. This shows your balanced hand, and 22 HCPs.

1c) 3NT. You again have a balanced hand. This time there are 25 HCPs plus 1 for the five-card diamond suit.

1d) 1♠. Although you have a strong hand—18 HCPs plus 1 for the five-card suit—it's not strong enough to open the bidding at the two level. Show your strength with your rebid.

1e) 2♠. With a choice of five-card suits to bid at the two level, start with the higher-ranking.

1f) 2♠. Although there are only 19 HCPs plus 2 for the six-card suit, this hands looks as though it belongs at the game level. You need hardly anything in partner's hand to take six spade tricks and four club tricks.

2a) 2NT. You can't pass partner's strong two-bid. Your first task is to send the message that you don't have a good hand, and you do this by responding 2NT.

2b) 3♥. With more than 6 points, your first priority is to show support for partner's suit. Once the suit is agreed, the partnership can work on deciding whether it belongs at the slam level or only at the game level.

2c) 2NT. The negative response of 2NT doesn't promise a balanced hand. It's an artificial bid to send the message to partner that you have less than 6 points. You may get to show your diamond suit later.

2d) 3♣. You don't have enough hearts to immediately support partner's suit. Instead, show a good suit of your own.

2e) 3NT. With a balanced hand of 9 HCPs, bid 3NT. 2NT would show 0–5 points.

2f) 2NT or 4♥. 2NT sends the message that you have a weak hand. A jump to game in partner's suit also sends this message, but shows good trump support. Make this bid only if you've discussed it with partner. You don't want partner getting too excited on this hand.

3a) **3NT.** Your 5 HCPs should be enough for game, since partner has at least 22 points. With no interest in a major suit fit, raise to game in notrump.

3b) **6NT.** Even if partner has only 22 points, your 11 HCPs gives the partnership a combined total of 33 points. That's enough to go to the slam level.

3c) **4NT.** With 10 HCPs, you need a little extra from partner for the slam zone. By raising beyond game, you're sending out an invitation. With only 22 points, partner will decline. With 23 or 24, partner will accept and carry on to slam.

4a) **Pass.** Partner is showing good trump support and a maximum-strength hand for an opening bid at the one level, 19–21 points. Your 7 points aren't enough to tempt you to bid higher.

4b) **6♠.** If partner has 19–21 points and you have 13—11 HCPs plus 2 for the six-card suit—the partnership belongs at the slam level. Time to see if you can take twelve tricks. Fans of the Blackwood Convention, which will be discussed later, could use it here.

4c) **5♠.** With only 11 HCPs and a five-card suit, you don't have quite enough to commit the partnership to the slam level after partner shows 19–21 points. Nonetheless, you can invite partner to bid a slam by raising beyond the game level. With only 19 points, partner will pass. With 20 or more, partner will accept.

Little Hands—
and
Big Bids

*"Don't hate yourself in the morning for the way
you played last night . . . sleep in till noon."*

Opening bids in a suit at the three level or higher actually show
hands too weak to open at the one level! It may seem strange, but
there's something to be said for making big bids with little hands.
Let's see why.

Striking First—Preemptive Bidding

Consider this hand. You're the dealer:

♠ 7
♥ K Q J 10 9 7 5
♦ 9 6 5
♣ 8 3

There are only six high card points, and even adding 3 points for the seven-card suit, you're well short of the requirements for a one-level opening bid. This hand has a lot of playing strength, if hearts is the trump suit. You should be able to take six heart tricks even if partner has nothing at all. You might like to send that message to partner.

At the same time, your hand is virtually worthless if the opponents get to name the trump suit, spades, for example. You aren't sure of taking even one trick on defense. It would be best if you could keep the opponents out of the auction, and get to name your suit as trump.

Hands like this are opened at the three level, 3♥. This is referred to as a *preemptive opening bid.*

The theory behind preemptive opening bids is that you describe your hand to partner—a weak hand with a long suit—while, at the same time, you make it difficult for the opponents to enter the auction.

What Opener Needs

To make an opening bid of 3♣, 3♦, 3♥, or 3♠ you need:

- A long, strong suit, typically seven cards in length.
- A weak hand, less than the values for a one-level opening bid.

The length and strength of your suit gives you some measure of safety. If the opponents double your contract for penalty, you can take a lot of tricks with your suit as trumps. Furthermore, if your hand is weak outside of your suit, the opponents can likely make a contract of their own. Whatever bonus they collect may not be enough to compensate them for the contract they would have made.

Here are some examples:

♠ 9 2
♥ 10
♦ A Q J 10 8 7 5
♣ J 4 3

3♦. A typical preemptive opening bid. A strong seven-card suit with little or no strength outside of the suit. You describe your hand to partner, and at the same time, take a lot of bidding room away from the opponents.

♠ A K J 8 7 6 4   3♠. Another good seven-card suit with no
♥ 10 2   defensive strength in any other suit.
♦ 5
♣ 8 4 2

♠ K 4   1♥. You don't make a preemptive bid just
♥ A Q 10 8 7 6 3   because you have a seven-card suit. This hand,
♦ Q 9 3   with 11 HCPs plus 3 points for the seven-card
♣ 3   suit, is strong enough for an opening bid at
                         the one level.

♠ J 9 7 6 4 3 2   Pass. Your suit isn't strong enough to make
♥ Q 8   a preemptive opening bid. You might not take
♦ 7 5   many tricks, and the opponents might double
♣ K 4   your contract for penalty. Also, you have some
                         high cards outside your suit which could be
useful if defending.

Preemptive opening bids are a very effective addition to your
toolbox, provided you use them with the right type of hand. By taking away a lot of bidding room from your opponents when they're
likely to have more high cards than your side, you may lead them
astray. They may reach the wrong contract; they may bid too much,
trying to prevent you from playing the contract; they may bid too
little, unaware of the potential of their combined hands.

What Responder Needs

An opening preemptive bid is very descriptive. It tells you that partner has a hand too weak to open at the one level, a good long suit,
and not much more. Partner's hand is not likely to take many tricks
unless the contract is played with partner's suit as trumps. Your side
may well be too high already, so you rarely bid unless you have good
support for partner's suit or a very strong hand of about 16 or more
points.

For example, suppose your partner opens the bidding 3♥, and
you hold one of the following hands:

♠ A J 9 6 2   Pass. You have 13 HCPs plus 1 point for
♥ 7   the five-card suit. Had partner opened the
♦ K Q 9 3   bidding at the one level, you would have
♣ Q J 4   enough to take the partnership to the game
                       level. Partner is showing less than the values
for an opening bid. There shouldn't be enough combined strength
for game. You're high enough already.

♠ A K 7 3   4♥. You have 17 HCPs, and game is likely
♥ 4 2   even if partner has only 9 or 10 points. Raise
♦ A 8 2   partner's seven-card suit rather than trying
♣ K Q J 8   something else, like 3NT. Partner has de-
                       scribed a hand that will take a lot of tricks if
hearts are trumps but very few otherwise.

♠ A K J 10 8 7   3♠. Partner's preemptive opening has made
♥ 10   things a little awkward for you, rather than
♦ A K Q 4   the opponents, on this hand. A new suit by
♣ 4 3   responder is forcing—if it's below the game
                       level. Perhaps partner can support your suit.

♠ 2   4♥. This may seem strange. Partner has a
♥ K J 6 5   weak hand, and you also have a weak hand!
♦ Q J 8 6 5   You do, however, have very good support for
♣ 10 8 2   partner's suit, and it's unlikely the opponents
                       can take more than five or six tricks against
your contract. Even though you don't expect to make your contract
of 4♥, think what the opponents might make. Partner has little or
no high card strength outside the heart suit, and neither do you.
The opponents can likely make a game contract playing in their
best trump suit—spades, perhaps—and may be able to make a small
slam or a grand slam. The penalty they can extract for defeating 4♥
will hardly compensate them for the game or slam bonus they will
have missed.

This last hand illustrates a tactic that often goes along with preemptive bidding, that of *sacrificing*. Sometimes your side should be willing to bid beyond what you can reasonably make. You do so in the hope that any penalty points you lose will be less than the score the opponents would receive for making their contract.

Higher Still

If opening the bidding at the three level is effective when you hold a seven-card suit, think how much fun you can have with an eight-card suit or longer. You can use these guidelines:

- With a weak hand but a good eight-card suit, open at the four level.
- With a weak hand but a good nine-card suit, open at the game level in a major or a minor.

For example:

♠ A Q J 8 6 5 4 2   4♠. By opening at the four level in your
♥ 10   eight-card suit, you make it very difficult for
♦ 5   the opponents to get into the auction.
♣ 8 6 2

♠ –   5♦. Now you're really getting up there. With
♥ J 4   your nine-card suit you expect to take eight
♦ K Q J 10 8 7 5 4 3   tricks all by yourself with diamonds as the
♣ 4 3   trump suit. In the meantime, who knows how
                                    many tricks your opponents might be able to
take if allowed to reach their optimum contract.

What the Defenders Need

When an opponent makes a preemptive bid, you can pass, make an overcall, or make a takeout double. Since you're committing the partnership to a lot of tricks when you bid, however, you need more strength than when you take action at the one level. Consider, for example, each of the following hands after the opponent on your right opens the bidding 3♥.

♠ K J 7 5   Pass. You might have made a takeout
♥ 10 2   double if your opponent opened the bidding
♦ A 8 6 4   1♥, but it would be very risky at the three level.
♣ K J 5   Partner will have to bid at least at the three
                level, and maybe the four level. If partner has
very little, your side will be much too high. This hand illustrates why
a preemptive opening bid is a good tactic. You know your opponents are trying to make things difficult for you, and on this hand it
looks as though they have succeeded.

♠ A K J 8 7 4   3♠. You would have preferred to open the
♥ J 5   bidding 1♠, but the auction is well beyond that
♦ A Q 4   now. With 15 HCPs and a good six-card suit,
♣ 4 3   you have enough to come into the auction
                with an overcall even though you're at the
                three level.

♠ A Q 10 8   Double. You have 16 HCPs plus 3 dummy
♥ 4   points for the singleton heart. While a take-
♦ K Q 7 3   out double commits your side to enter the bid-
♣ K Q 10 6   ding at the three level or higher, you have too
                much to pass.

Utilizing the Two Level—Weak Two Bids

Some players like to take the concept of preemptive opening bids a
bit further. Rather than waiting for a seven-card suit that they can
open at the three level, they prefer to start even lower—with a six-
card suit at the two level.

The Weak Two-Bid

Instead of using the entire two level to show strong hands, some
partnerships use an opening bid of 2♦, 2♥, or 2♠ to show a weak

hand with a good six-card suit. This is referred to as a *weak two-bid*. For example:

♠ A Q J 10 7 3
♥ 8 3
♦ 7 4
♣ 10 9 7

If the partnership uses weak two-bids, this hand would be opened 2♠. As you can see, a weak two-bid is similar to a preemptive three-level opening except that it shows only a good six-card suit, with less than the values for an opening bid at the one level.

In order to free up the 2♦, 2♥, and 2♠ bids, all strong hands of 22 or more points are opened with an artificial forcing bid of 2♣. For example:

♠ A K Q 10 7 3
♥ A 3
♦ K 4
♣ A K 7

This hand would be opened 2♣. The 2♣ bid says nothing about playing in clubs, it merely sends the message: "Partner, I have a very strong hand." Opener plans to show the real suit on the next round of bidding.

Weak two-bids are very popular in North America, especially among club and tournament players. They can be effective, but like all such bids, they require some extra effort from the partnership to avoid any misunderstandings during the auction. The partnership is unlikely to end up with a good result, for example, if one member thinks that a 2♠ bid shows a very strong hand while the other thinks that it shows a very weak hand!

Responding to a Weak Two-Bid

Most partnerships respond to weak two-bids in a manner similar to responding to three-level preemptive bids. Responder passes except with a very strong hand or with good support for partner's suit. Usually, 2NT is used as an artificial forcing response, asking opener to further describe the hand. There are a number of different styles, and if you plan to use weak two-bids with your partner, you'll need to sit down and discuss the various sequences.

Responding to an Opening 2♣ Bid

If your partnership uses weak two-bids, an opening bid of 2♣ is artificial, saying nothing except that opener has a very strong hand. To avoid using up too much bidding room, most partnerships play that a response of 2♦ is also an artificial bid, either a negative response—similar to the 2NT response to a strong two-bid—or a *waiting bid*, giving opener a chance to describe the hand. A typical auction might sound like this:

	OPENER		RESPONDER
	♠ 3		♠ K J 8 5 2
	♥ A K Q 10 8 5		♥ 7 3
	♦ A K Q J		♦ 8 2
	♣ Q 8		♣ J 9 4 2

2♣	*I have a strong hand . . .*	2♦	*Tell me more.*
2♥	*. . . with a heart suit . . .*	2♠	*How about spades?*
3♦	*. . . and a diamond suit.*	3♥	*I think I prefer hearts to diamonds.*
4♥	*Okay.*	Pass	*I have nothing more to say.*

Notice that opener was able to show the strong hand with a heart suit by the time the auction reached 2♥. By making use of the artificial 2♣ opening and artificial 2♦ response, the partnership was in the same position as those using strong two-bids, who would have opened 2♥ originally. The advantage of this style is that an immediate opening bid of 2♥ has now been freed up for use as a weak two-bid.

Using weak two-bids and an artificial 2♣ bid for all strong hands adds some complexity to the partnership's bidding methods. The benefit is that you can now make a descriptive and "mini-preemptive" opening bid at the two level. It provides another tool for entering the auction before the opponents start bidding, putting your side at a competitive advantage.

It's Never Too Late—Jump Overcalls

Preemptive bids are most effective when you get to use them before either opponent has had an opportunity to bid. The opponents have to start their first exchange of information at a high level. Although it's less effective, you can still interrupt the opponents' auction after it's started.

Double Jump Overcalls

Most partnerships play that an overcall that skips two levels of bidding shows a hand similar to a preemptive opening bid. For example, suppose the opponent on your right opens the bidding 1♦, and you hold this hand:

♠ 8 2
♥ K Q J 9 7 6 3
♦ 9
♣ J 10 7

A jump to 3♥, rather than an overcall of 1♥ or 2♥, can be used to describe this hand to partner, and at the same time, take a lot of bidding room away from the opponents.

This bid is a bit more risky than an opening bid of 3♥. Your left-hand opponent has heard the opening bid of 1♦, and therefore knows something about the combined strength of the hands. Using this knowledge, your left-hand opponent is in a position to double your contract for penalties with a few high cards and some heart length. The longer and stronger your suit, the less chance of this happening. In many auctions, the disruptive nature of a preemptive bid can provide the opponents with a profound challenge.

Weak Jump Overcalls

Not all partnerships have similar agreements when it comes to the meaning of a single jump overcall, jumping to 2♥ over the opponent's 1♦ opening bid, for example. Some players like to use this bid to show a hand too strong to make a simple overcall of 1♥, usually a hand with a good six-card suit and about 17 or more points. This style is referred to as *strong jump overcalls*. Other partnerships prefer a style of *intermediate jump overcalls*, where a jump overcall shows a good six-card or longer suit with about 14–16 points.

The style that's become popular in recent years is *weak jump overcalls*. Rather like the weak two-bid, a jump overcall shows a weak hand with a good six-card or longer suit. For example, consider these hands after the bidding is opened 1♦ on your right:

♠ A Q J 9 7 5
♥ 9 3
♦ 6 4
♣ J 8 5

2♠. Like a weak two-bid, the jump overcall shows a good suit but little defensive strength outside the suit. It would be dangerous to bid 3♠ with only a six-card suit, so the weak jump overcall allows you to interfere with the opponents auction without too much risk for your side. In addition, you describe your hand to partner, who can take appropriate action.

♠ 9 7 5
♥ 2
♦ J 8
♣ K Q J 9 7 6 3

3♣. This is a better way to show a weak hand than having to jump all the way to 4♣ with only a seven-card suit. You use up a fair amount of the opponents' bidding room in the auction while ending up at a reasonably safe level with your suit as trump.

♠ K 9
♥ A Q 10 8 3
♦ 8 6 4
♣ K 7 4

1♥. With this hand, you would make your normal overcall at the one level. You have neither a long suit nor a weak hand. Using jump overcalls allows the partnership to distinguish between two types of hands: those with a long suit and a weak hand, and those with a good suit and more general high card strength.

Responding to Jump Overcalls

You treat partner's jump overcall in the same manner as a preemptive opening bid. Unless you have good support for partner's suit, you shouldn't bid without considerable strength, about 16 or more points. Partner's bid shows less than the values for an opening bid. You won't be missing a game contract if you have a hand of opening bid strength. The preemptive jump overcall has already disrupted the opponents' auction, so you shouldn't risk putting the partnership in any more danger. There's one exception. You may want to take further bidding room away from the opponents by making a "sacrifice" bid. Let's look at some examples after the auction starts off like this:

LHO	PARTNER	RHO	YOU
1♦	2♥	Pass	?

♠ K Q 8 5
♥ 8 3
♦ K Q 6 2
♣ K 10 3

Pass. Your high cards may help partner take eight tricks in the 2♥ contract, but not much more. The partnership belongs in partscore, and may already be too high.

♠ A K 9 6
♥ J 7 3
♦ 4
♣ K Q J 7 4

4♥. With this hand, you have reasonable expectations that partner can make a 4♥ contract. You have a fit with partner's six-card suit, a singleton, and 14 HCPs. Partner's descriptive bid has let you know which trump suit is best for the partnership.

♠ 9
♥ Q 10 6 2
♦ 10 5 4
♣ Q 9 7 5 2

4♥. Here you're bidding out of weakness rather than strength. You have an excellent fit with partner's suit, but it doesn't look like either of you has much defensive strength against any contract the opponents choose— 4♠ or 6♠, for example. By taking more bidding room away from your opponents, perhaps they'll misjudge, and miss their best contract. You're willing to sacrifice the penalty points you'll lose for being defeated in your contract. You hope the penalty will be less than the bonus the opponents would get if left to find their best contract.

Summary

A preemptive opening bid at the three level (3♣, 3♦, 3♥, or 3♠) shows:

- A long, strong suit, typically seven cards in length.
- A weak hand, less than the values for a one-level opening bid.

With a longer suit, you can open at a higher level:

- With a weak hand but a good eight-card suit, open at the four level.
- With a weak hand but a good nine-card suit, open at the game level.

If your partnership uses weak two-bids, all strong hands are opened 2♣, and an opening bid of 2♦, 2♥, or 2♠ shows:

- A good six-card suit.
- A weak hand, typically 5–10 HCPs.

After the opponents have opened the bidding, a weak hand with a good long suit can be shown by:

- Jumping two levels of bidding when overcalling the suit.
- Jumping one level of bidding when overcalling the suit, if the partnership uses weak jump overcalls.

When partner makes a preemptive bid, you should generally pass unless you have about 16 or more points or you have good support for partner's suit. With good support and a weak hand, you can consider raising partner's suit as a sacrifice against the opponents' possible contract.

Exercises

1. What would be your opening bid with each of the following hands?

a) ♠ 5
   ♥ 7 2
   ♦ J 8 4
   ♣ A J 10 9 7 6 4

b) ♠ −
   ♥ K Q 10 9 7 6 4 2
   ♦ 9 4
   ♣ 10 6 3

c) ♠ A Q J 9 7 4 2
   ♥ Q 4
   ♦ 5
   ♣ K 7 5

d) ♠ 9 7
   ♥ A Q 10 9 7 3
   ♦ 6 5
   ♣ Q 10 5

e) ♠ Q 6
   ♥ 2
   ♦ J 9 6 5 4 3 2
   ♣ A J 4

f) ♠ A K Q 7 5
   ♥ 7
   ♦ A K J 10 7
   ♣ A 5

2. What would you bid with each of the following hands after the bidding starts off:

LHO	PARTNER	RHO	YOU
1♦	Pass	1♥	?

a) ♠ K J 10 8 7
   ♥ A 3
   ♦ 9 4
   ♣ A 10 9 3

b) ♠ K Q J 10 8 3
   ♥ 7 4
   ♦ 5 3
   ♣ J 10 2

c) ♠ A Q J 8 6 5 4
   ♥ 10
   ♦ J 9 3
   ♣ 7 6

3. What would you bid with each of the following hands after the bidding proceeds:

LHO	PARTNER	RHO	YOU
1♥	2♠ (weak)	3♥	?

a) ♠ 7 3
   ♥ Q J 9 5
   ♦ A J 4
   ♣ K Q 7 4

b) ♠ A J 7 2
   ♥ 4
   ♦ A K J 7 2
   ♣ Q 9 3

c) ♠ K 9 6 2
   ♥ 10 2
   ♦ J 9 8 7 4 2
   ♣ 7 3

4.   What would you bid with each of the following hands if the bidding goes:

LHO	PARTNER	RHO	YOU
3♥	Pass	Pass	?

a) ♠ Q J 7
   ♥ Q 4 3
   ♦ K J 7 6 2
   ♣ A 10

b) ♠ A Q
   ♥ 7 4
   ♦ 5 3
   ♣ A K J 10 7 5 2

c) ♠ K Q 9 3
   ♥ 6
   ♦ A J 10 2
   ♣ K J 6 5

Answers to Exercises

1a) 3♣. You have a good seven-card suit and only 6 HCPs. This is an ideal hand to open with a preemptive three-level bid.

1b) 4♥. With an eight-card suit and less than the values for an opening bid at the one level, you can open at the four level.

1c) 1♠. Although you have a seven-card suit, you have 12 HCPs. Counting 3 length points for the seven-card suit, you have enough to open the bidding at the one level.

1d) 2♥ or **Pass**. If your partnership uses weak two-bids, you would open this hand 2♥, showing a good six-card suit but less than the values for an opening bid. Otherwise, you would simply pass.

1e) **Pass**. Although you have a weak hand and a seven-card suit, your suit isn't strong and most of your high cards are located outside the suit. This isn't the right type of hand for a preemptive opening bid.

1f) 2♣ or 2♠. This hand has the strength for a strong forcing opening bid. If you use weak two-bids, all such hands are opened with 2♣. If you use strong two-bids, you would open at the two level in the higher-ranking of your two five-card suits, 2♠.

2a) 1♠. This hand is worth a simple overcall at the one level, showing your five-card suit and your desire to compete for the contract.

2b) 2♠ or 1♠. If your partnership uses weak jump overcalls, you would jump to 2♠ with this hand to show a long spade suit with little strength outside of the suit. If this isn't your style, you could simply overcall 1♠ with this hand.

2c) 3♠. With a good seven-card suit but a weak hand, you can make a double jump overcall with this hand. Some players might make a weak jump overcall of 2♠ with this hand, but you take up more of the opponents' bidding room by jumping to the three level.

3a) **Pass**. Although you have the values for an opening bid, this isn't the time to say anything. Partner is showing a weak hand with a long spade suit. Your best tactic is to keep quiet, and defend against whatever contract the opponents reach.

3b) **4♠**. With 15 HCPs, a singleton and good support for partner's suit, you should expect to make game opposite partner's weak jump overcall.

3c) **4♠**. Here you're bidding out of weakness, rather than strength. You don't expect to make 10 tricks in your 4♠ contract, but any bonus the opponents receive for defeating your contract should be less than the score they would get if they play the hand in their best spot.

4a) **Pass**. Although you have the values for an opening bid at the one level, the auction is too high to enter at this point. You don't have a good suit to overcall nor the right type of hand for a takeout double. You'll have to hope that you can defeat the opponents' contract.

4b) **4♣**. With 14 HCPs and a good seven-card suit, you don't want to let the opponents play in their best suit. You would prefer being able to introduce your club suit at a lower level, but now you have no such choice.

4c) **Double**. This is a takeout double. You have good support for the unbid suits and your hand is worth 17 points—14 HCPs plus 3 dummy points for the singleton heart. That's enough to risk coming into the auction, even at this level.

Part 7

CONVENTIONS

Stayman, Blackwood— and All That

"The convention system has its faults, of course, but I do not know a better method for choosing a presidential nominee."

— HARRY S TRUMAN

In this book, you've already seen some examples of how bridge partnerships can assign artificial, or conventional, meanings to certain bids. A conventional bid sends a special message to partner; one that has nothing to do with the bid itself. Examples discussed so far include: the use of 2NT as an artificial, negative response to a strong two-bid; the use of an opening 2♣ bid to show a strong hand when employing weak two-bids; the use of the cue bid of the opponents' suit in response to an overcall or takeout double as a forcing response.

Tournament bridge players use a number of *conventions*, or gadgets, for special types of hands. This requires some extra memory work by the partnership, but sometimes results in increased accuracy in getting to the best contract. Some of these conventions are common practice among bridge players at all levels of the game. In this chapter, we'll take a look at a few of the favorites.

A convention involves the use of artificial bids. This is different from a bidding *style*. A bidding style sticks closely to the natural meaning of a bid. Whether your partnership style is four-card majors or five-card majors, an opening bid of 1♥ shows a desire to play with hearts as the trump suit. Similarly, whether you play weak two-bids or strong two-bids, an opening bid of 2♠ shows a spade suit. Conventional bids are, as they say, a horse of a different color.

The Stayman Convention— Do You Have a Four-Card Major?

When partner opens the bidding 1NT, responder wants to find a major suit fit whenever possible. With a six-card or longer major suit, responder knows there's a fit, and can sign off in partscore by bidding the suit at the two level, or in game by bidding the suit at the four level. With a five-card suit, responder can jump to the three level to ask opener to bid 3NT with only two cards in the suit, or raise to game with three-card or longer support. Now responder is left with the challenge of what to do holding only a four-card major suit.

The Stayman Convention

Suppose partner opens the bidding 1NT, and this is your hand:

> ♠ K J 7 5
> ♥ A Q 4 2
> ♦ 10 3 2
> ♣ 7 5

Holding 10 HCPs, your target is the game level. You'd like to play in an eight-card major suit fit if the partnership has one. If not, 3NT should be the best contract.

Most partnerships use the *Stayman Convention* in this situation. A response of 2♣ asks opener to show a four-card major suit. This is a convention in the truest sense of the word, since the 2♣ bid has nothing to do with clubs. It's an artificial forcing bid that sends a specific message to partner.

By using 2♣ in this manner, the partnership can no longer use it as a sign-off bid, like 2♦, 2♥, or 2♠. That's the down side, but there are many advantages available through use of the Stayman Convention.

Responding to Stayman

When partner responds to your 1NT opening bid with 2♣, the Stayman Convention, you rebid as follows:

2♦   "I have no four-card or longer major suit."

2♥   "I have a four-card or longer heart suit."

2♠   "I have a four-card or longer spade suit."

This answers partner's question. Let's look at some examples after the auction starts this way:

LHO	PARTNER	RHO	YOU
			1NT
Pass	2♣ (Stayman)	Pass	?

♠ A 4 3
♥ K J 10
♦ Q 4
♣ A Q 9 8 3

2♦. Partner has asked you to show a four-card major suit if you have one. When you don't, you rebid 2♦. Like the 2♣ bid, 2♦ is a conventional bid having nothing to do with diamonds. It simply sends a message back to partner that you don't have four or more cards in a major suit.

♠ Q 10 6 3
♥ K 8
♦ A K 6 4
♣ K J 9

2♠. With this hand, you would tell partner about your four-card spade suit. Partner isn't interested in whether or not it's a good suit, only that you have four of them!

♠ A 9 6 2
♥ K 10 7 5
♦ A 4
♣ A J 8

2♥. With a choice of four-card suits, you can bid the suits "up the line," showing the hearts first. Some partnerships have specific agreements on which suit to show first, but it doesn't really matter. We'll bid up the line.

Rebidding after Stayman

Once opener replies to the Stayman convention, responder can decide what to do next based on the new information. Here are some examples after the auction begins this way:

LHO	PARTNER	RHO	YOU
	1NT	Pass	2♣
Pass	2♥	Pass	?

♠ K J 7 5
♥ A Q 4 2
♦ 10 3 2
♣ 7 5

4♥. Holding 10 HCPs, and with partner showing at least 16 points, the partnership belongs at the game level. Now that you have found an eight-card major suit fit, you can put the partnership in the best game contract.

Had partner responded 2♦, you would put the partnership in a contract of 3NT, since there would be no eight-card major suit fit.

♠ K J 7 5
♥ A 8 4 2
♦ 10 3 2
♣ 7 5

3♥. On this hand you have only 8 HCPs, enough to invite opener to a game contract. You start by using the Stayman Convention to find out if opener has a four-card major suit.
When opener shows a four-card heart suit, you can raise to invite opener to continue on with the top of the notrump range. Holding only 16 points, opener can pass, and the partnership will stop in partscore.

♠ K J 7 5
♥ 4 2
♦ A 10 3 2
♣ K 7 5

3NT. Since you hold 11 HCPs, the partnership belongs at the game level. You respond 2♣ to ask if partner has a major suit, in case there's an eight-card spade fit—you don't need both major suits to use the Stayman convention. Partner shows you a four-card heart suit, which isn't the suit in which you're interested, so you put the partnership in a 3NT contract. If partner turns out to have both major suits, partner can now bid 4♠, knowing you must have been interested in spades once you don't support hearts. Without a four-card spade suit, partner will pass, and you'll end up in 3NT.

♠ K J 7 5
♥ 4 2
♦ A 10 3 2
♣ 10 7 5

2NT. This is similar to the previous hand. You have spades and partner has hearts—no eight-card major suit fit. You have only enough strength to invite partner to the game level. Partner can accept the invitation holding the top of the range for a 1NT opening bid. Otherwise, partner can pass, and the partnership will rest in partscore.

As can be seen from the above examples, the Stayman Convention can be used by responder with both invitational hands in the 8–9 point range, and with hands of 10 or more points. It's generally not a good idea to use Stayman with less than 8 points because you may end up too high when you don't find a major suit fit. For example, you should pass if partner opens the bidding 1NT when you hold this hand:

♠ 7 5
♥ K Q 8 3
♦ 9 4 2
♣ 10 8 6 4

If you were to respond 2♣, you'd be okay if opener rebid 2♥—you could pass, and the partnership would be in the best partscore. If opener were to respond 2♦ or 2♠, however, you might be in trouble. If you now bid 2NT, partner will assume that's an invitational bid showing 8 or 9 points, and may continue on to game. Better to stop in 1NT than risk ending up in a game contract when you have only 5 points!

More about Stayman

The Stayman Convention can also be used when you have an invitational strength hand of 8 or 9 points and a five-card or longer major
suit. For example:

♠ K J 10 8 4
♥ 9 3
♦ K 9 3
♣ J 10 5

With 8 HCPs and a five-card suit, you have too much to sign off in
partscore by responding 2♠ when partner opens the bidding 1NT.
On the other hand, you aren't strong enough to commit the partnership to game by bidding 3♠, asking opener to choose between
3NT and 4♠. You could show an invitational hand by raising to 2NT,
but you might miss an eight-card or longer fit in spades.

The way to handle this type of hand is by starting off with the
Stayman response of 2♣. Partner will make the normal reply, showing a four-card major or bidding 2♦ without one. If opener does bid
2♠, showing a four-card suit, you can make an invitational raise to
3♠. If, instead, opener rebids 2♦ or 2♥, you can now make an invitational rebid of 2♠.

How would opener recognize that your 2♠ bid shows an invitational strength hand? If you had a weak hand with a spade suit, you
would have signed off by bidding 2♠ right away. With a hand of 10 or
more points, you would originally respond 3♠ with a five-card suit or
4♠ with a six-card or longer suit. By using the Stayman Convention
first, you're showing something in-between—an invitational strength
hand with a spade suit.

Auctions such as this take some practice. It may be easier for you
to simply raise to 2NT with hands like this until you've had an opportunity to discuss such sequences with your partner. That's one of
the troubles with conventions—they sometimes leave you with more
unanswered questions than before you started using them!

... And Yet More Stayman

You can also use the Stayman Convention when partner opens the bidding 2NT. In this case, a response of 3♣ is the Stayman Convention, and opener rebids 3♦ with no major suit, or 3♥ or 3♠ to show a four-card or longer suit.

Once you know how to use Stayman over 1NT, you might as well use it over 2NT. There's nothing new to learn!

The Blackwood Convention— How Many Aces Do You Have?

When slam bidding was discussed earlier in the book, it was mentioned that the partnership didn't want to be missing two aces when it undertook a small slam contract or even one ace in a grand slam contract. You don't want the opponents in a position to defeat your slam contract on the opening lead!

For example, suppose you pick up the following hand:

♠ K Q 9 4
♥ A K Q 7 5
♦ K Q 7
♣ 9

The bidding starts this way:

LHO	PARTNER	RHO	YOU
	1♣	Pass	1♥
Pass	2♥	Pass	?

Partner has shown at least 13 points, and you have 19 HCPs plus 1 for the five-card suit, putting the combined total in the slam zone. You have also found out about your heart fit. At this point, you could jump to 6♥, but it would be a shame if the opponents were to take the first two tricks with aces, before you had a chance to take your tricks.

In the 1930's, a fellow named Easley Blackwood popularized a method for finding out how many aces the partnership holds—and was immortalized in the bridge world when the convention was named after him.

The Blackwood Convention

The mechanics of the *Blackwood Convention* are quite straightforward. Once the partnership has agreed on a trump suit and there appears to be enough combined strength for a slam level contract, a bid of **4NT asks partner to show the number of aces held.** Partner responds as follows:

5♣ No aces (or all four aces).
5♦ One ace.
5♥ Two aces.
5♠ Three aces.

Now you can add up the number of aces held by partner to those that you hold, and decide whether or not it's safe to bid a slam. Here are some examples of how the partnership can put the Blackwood Convention to work:

OPENER	RESPONDER
♠ A J 5	♠ K Q 9 4
♥ J 10 8 4	♥ A K Q 7 5
♦ 5	♦ K Q 7
♣ K Q J 6 3	♣ 9

1♣	*I have an opening bid.*	1♥	*I know we're headed toward slam, but first we should find our fit.*
2♥	*I have support for your hearts and a minimum-strength hand.*	4NT	*Good, we've found our fit. How many aces do you have, partner?*
5♦	*I have one ace.*	5♥	*Too bad. We have only two of the four aces. The opponents can take the first two tricks.*
Pass	*You're the captain.*		

OPENER	RESPONDER
♠ A J 5	♠ K Q 9 4
♥ J 10 8 4	♥ A K Q 7 5
♦ 5 4	♦ K Q 7
♣ A Q J 6	♣ 9

1♣	*I have another opening bid.*	1♥	*I still need to find a fit before thinking about bidding a slam.*
2♥	*I like your hearts but I have only a minimum-strength hand.*	4NT	*Now that I know where we're going to play. It's time to haul out the Blackwood Convention.*
5♥	*This time I have two aces.*	6♥	*You have two and I have one. That leaves only one for the opponents. Our slam should stand a good chance.*
Pass	*Good luck, partner!*		

After 4NT

After bidding 4NT, and finding out how many aces partner holds, responder can sign off in the agreed trump suit below the slam level if the partnership doesn't hold enough aces or bid to the slam level if there are enough aces. If the partnership holds all the aces, and responder is interested in bidding a grand slam, responder can bid 5NT to ask partner to show the number of kings held. Partner shows the number of kings in a similar fashion to showing the number of aces:

6♣   No aces.
6♦   One ace.
6♥   Two aces.
6♠   Three aces.
6NT Four aces.

For example:

OPENER	RESPONDER
♠ A J 5 3	♠ K Q 10 8 4 2
♥ J 10 8	♥ A K
♦ A 10 7 4	♦ K 9
♣ K 3	♣ A Q 7

1♦	*I like opening the bidding.*	1♠	*Let's see what partner thinks about spades.*
2♠	*I like your spades, but, as usual, I don't have any extra strength.*	4NT	*But I do! We're headed for the slam level.*
5♥	*Two aces, partner.*	5NT	*That takes care of all the aces. How about kings?*
6♦	*Only one of those.*	7♠	*I'll bet it's the ♣K. I think we can take all the tricks.*
Pass	*This will be one to tell the grandchildren about.*		

When Not to Use Blackwood

While the Blackwood Convention is very useful, it tells you only how many aces partner holds, not which aces. If finding out the number of aces may not do you any good, you shouldn't be using the Blackwood Convention. For example, suppose partner opens the bidding 1♠, and this is your hand:

♠ Q J 10 6 5
♥ A K Q J 5
♦ K Q 7
♣ —

You have the values to want to take the partnership to the slam level, but bidding 4NT to find out how many aces partner has is unlikely to do much good. If partner shows one ace, it might be the ♣A. That won't do you any good because it's opposite your void. If partner shows two aces, they might be the ♣A and ♦A. You could still be missing the ♠A and ♠K.

There are methods to deal with hands like this, but they're beyond the scope of this book—and beyond the grasp of most partnerships. For now, it's easier to simply bid the slam, and take your chances.

The Gerber Convention

The Blackwood Convention is used only after a trump suit has been agreed upon. If partner opens the bidding 1NT or 2NT, a response of 4NT is an invitational raise, showing a hand too strong to stop at the game level, but not quite strong enough to bid slam unless partner has a little extra strength.

If you need to know how many aces partner has after an opening notrump bid, you can use the *Gerber Convention*. A response of 4♣ asks partner how many aces are held, and partner responds as follows:

4♦   No aces (or all four).
4♥   One ace.
4♠   Two aces.
4NT Three aces.

For example, suppose partner opens the bidding 1NT and this is your hand:

> ♠ 8
> ♥ A 5 3
> ♦ K Q J 10 8 7 5
> ♣ A 5

With 14 HCPs plus 3 points for the seven-card suit, you have enough to take partnership to the slam level. In case you're missing two aces, however, you can check by responding 4♣. If partner shows no aces by responding 4♦, you would stop in 5♦. If partner responds 4♥, showing one ace, you would bid 6♦. If partner shows both missing aces, you could consider a grand slam—a bid of 5♣ would now ask for kings, and the responses follow the same pattern.

The Unusual Notrump—
Which Minor Suit Do You Prefer?

Another popular convention is used when you hold a hand like this, and the opponent on your right opens the bidding 1♥:

♠ 7
♥ 8
♦ K Q J 10 5
♣ K Q J 8 7 6

You could overcall in your long suit, 2♣, but if the opponents then bid up to 4♥, you would have a difficult decision to make as to whether or not to show your other suit by bidding 5♦. That could work out well. But if partner prefers clubs to diamonds and bids 6♣, the partnership is likely to be much too high. It would be nice if you could show both your suits at once, and let partner choose the trump suit before the auction gets too high.

The Unusual Notrump

When the opponents open the bidding in a major suit, it's not often that you hold a balanced hand with 22–24 points which you would like to show by overcalling 2NT. Many partnerships prefer to use the jump overcall to 2NT to show both minor suits, asking partner to choose one. It's like a takeout double, but for only two suits. This is referred to as the *unusual (two) notrump*.

To use the unusual notrump, you should have at least five cards in each of the minor suits with very little strength outside the two suits. Partner can then judge how high to bid depending on the support held in your suits. For example, suppose the auction starts out as follows:

LHO	PARTNER	RHO	YOU
1♠	2NT	Pass	?

♠ Q 9 8 4
♥ K J 7 6 3
♦ 7 3 2
♣ 4

3♦. This isn't the type of hand partner was hoping you would hold, but partner has asked you to choose a minor suit, and you should do so. Fortunately, partner will have at least five diamonds, so there will be some measure of safety at the three level.

♠ 8 7 6 2
♥ 4
♦ A J 3
♣ K 9 7 4 3

5♣. Here you have an excellent fit with one of partner's suits and some valuable high cards in partner's other suit. There's a good chance that you can take 11 tricks with clubs as the trump suit. You should make this bid even if the opponent on your right bids something—4♠, for example.

Covering More Ground

Some partnerships extend the use of the unusual notrump to show the two lower-ranking unbid suits rather than specifically the minor suits. It still carries its old meaning when the opponents open the bidding 1♥ or 1♠ because the lowest-ranking unbid suits are clubs and diamonds. If the opponents open the bidding 1♦, however, a jump to 2NT could be used to show this hand:

♠ 8
♥ K Q J 8 4
♦ 3
♣ K J 10 8 4 2

The two lower-ranking unbid suits are now clubs and hearts. As usual, you should discuss the use of any conventional bids very carefully with your partner before you adopt them. The partnership needs to be on the same wavelength.

Summary

When partner opens the bidding 1NT, a response of 2♣ can be used as the Stayman Convention, asking opener to show a four-card or longer major suit. Opener responds as follows:

2♦   No four-card or longer major suit.
2♥   A four-card or longer heart suit.
2♠   A four-card or longer spade suit.

Responder can then use this information to help decide on the best contract for the partnership.

When the partnership has agreed on a trump suit and is interested in going to the slam level, a bid of 4NT is the Blackwood Convention and asks partner to show the number of aces held as follows:

5♣   No aces (or all four).
5♦   One ace.
5♥   Two aces.
5♠   Three aces.

You can then use this information to decide whether the partnership belongs in a slam contract or should stop short of slam because too many aces are missing.

When the opponents open the bidding in a major suit, a jump overcall of 2NT (unusual notrump) can be used to ask partner to bid a minor suit at the three level or higher.

The are many popular conventions which a partnership can add to their bidding methods. You should be careful, however, to discuss each one very thoroughly with your partner before using it. You can usually get by quite well without conventional bids, and any potential benefits may be lost if either partner becomes confused about the meaning of the bids.

Exercises

1. What would you rebid on each of these hands after the bidding starts:

LHO	PARTNER	RHO	YOU
			1NT
Pass	2♣(Stayman)	Pass	?

a) ♠ K Q 7 3
   ♥ J 5
   ♦ A J 10 8
   ♣ A Q 4

b) ♠ A Q
   ♥ K 10 9 5 3
   ♦ K 9 6
   ♣ K J 5

c) ♠ A K J
   ♥ K Q 4
   ♦ 7 6
   ♣ K J 6 4 2

2. What would you bid on each of these hands after the bidding starts:

LHO	PARTNER	RHO	YOU
	1NT	Pass	2♣
Pass	2♠	Pass	?

a) ♠ A 10 6 4
   ♥ K 3
   ♦ K 9 7
   ♣ J 8 5 2

b) ♠ 9 5
   ♥ A Q 6 2
   ♦ 9 7
   ♣ K J 8 6 3

c) ♠ K 10 9 3
   ♥ 8 4
   ♦ A 7 6 3
   ♣ J 10 8

3. What would you bid on each of these hands after the auction begins:

LHO	PARTNER	RHO	YOU
		Pass	1♦
Pass	1♠	Pass	3♠
Pass	4NT (Blackwood)	Pass	?

a) ♠ A Q 7 2   b) ♠ K Q 10 3   c) ♠ A 10 9 3
   ♥ K 4   ♥ 2   ♥ A 3
   ♦ A K 9 6 3   ♦ K Q 10 9 7   ♦ A Q 10 7 6 3
   ♣ 10 5   ♣ K Q 3   ♣ 5

4. What would you do with each of these hands after the bidding starts:

LHO	PARTNER	RHO	YOU
		1♥	?

a) ♠ 2   b) ♠ 8   c) ♠ 9 3
   ♥ 3   ♥ 9 4   ♥ 4
   ♦ K J 9 8 6 4   ♦ A K J 8 7 2 ♦ K 9 7 5 3
   ♣ A J 10 9 6   ♣ K Q 7 3   ♣ Q J 10 8 4

Answers to Exercises

1a) **2♠**. Partner's 2♣ response asks you to show a four-card major suit.

1b) **2♥**. Here you have a heart suit to show partner. The 2♣ response asks for a four-card or longer major suit.

1c) **2♦**. With no four-card major suit you, respond 2♦. This is a conventional response, and has nothing to do with your holding in the diamond suit.

2a) **4♠**. With 11 HCPs you want to get the partnership to a game level contract. By responding 2♣ you've found that the partnership has an eight-card major suit fit. You now know everything you need to place the contract.

2b) **3NT**. With 10 HCPs plus 1 point for the five-card suit, you have enough to take the partnership to the game level. By responding 2♣, you've found out that partner has a four-card spade suit. That isn't what you were looking for. Since there's no major suit fit, put partner in game in notrump.

2c) **3♠**. You have uncovered the major suit fit, but you don't have enough to commit the partnership to the game level. Raise to the three level to invite opener to carry on with the top of the range for a 1NT opening bid.

3a) **5♥**. Partner is using the Blackwood Convention to find out how many aces you have. With two, you respond 5♥.

3b) **5♣**. On this hand you have no aces for partner. You show this by making the cheapest possible response, 5♣.

3c) **5♠**. With three aces to show partner, you respond 5♠. After a while, you won't have to count on your fingers!

4a) **2NT**. Here is your opportunity to bid the unusual notrump, asking partner to pick a minor. Let's hope partner doesn't have only one card in each suit.

4b) **2♦**. Use the unusual notrump only when you have at least five cards in each minor suit. With this hand, you have a definite preference for diamonds. Don't leave the choice of suit to partner.

4c) Pass. There is a limit to how frisky you can get. Bidding 2NT, and committing the partnership to the three level in a minor suit, would be brave—but reckless!

Glossary

adequate trump support   A holding of enough cards in partner's suit to guarantee a combined eight-card fit. For example, if the partnership uses five-card majors, three-card support is adequate to raise.

artificial bid   A call during the auction which, by partnership agreement, carries a special message unrelated to the suit bid. For example, the 2♣ response to 1NT, used for the Stayman Convention, doesn't suggest clubs as the trump suit.

auction   The bidding by the four players to decide on the contract.

balanced hand   A hand containing no voids, no singletons, and at most one doubleton. There are three balanced hand patterns: 4-3-3-3, 4-4-3-2, and 5-3-3-2.

better minor   Opening the bidding in the longer minor suit, or the stronger of two equal-length minor suits, when holding no five-card or longer major suit.

Blackwood Convention   A bid of 4NT, after a trump suit has been agreed upon, to ask partner to show the number of aces held.

controls   Holdings that prevent the other side from taking one or two immediate tricks in a suit. An ace or a void is a first-round control. A king or a singleton is a second-round control.

convention   A bid or play that carries a special meaning for the partnership. For example, the response of 2♣ to an opening bid of 1NT (Stayman Convention).

cue bid   A forcing bid in a suit which the bidder cannot want to suggest as the trump suit. Usually used to show a strong hand when responding to an overcall or a takeout double.

distribution   The number of cards held in each suit in a player's hand. Points for distribution are added to the high card points when valuing a hand.

doubleton   A holding of two cards in a suit.

dummy points   Points used in place of length points when valuing a hand in support of partner's suit: void, 5 points; singleton, 3 points; doubleton, 1 point.

eight-card fit   A combined partnership holding of eight or more cards in a suit. An eight-card fit makes a suitable trump suit.

five-card majors   A bidding style in which the opening bidder must have at least five cards in a major to bid the suit.

forcing raise   A bidding style in which a jump raise of opener's suit to the three level commits the partnership to a game contract.

forcing bid   A bid that partner isn't expected to pass.

four-card majors   A bidding style in which the opening bidder only needs four cards in a major to bid the suit.

gambling 3NT (overcall)   A bid of 3NT on a hand containing a long solid suit, rather than the traditional 25–27 HCPs for an opening 3NT.

game   A contract with a trick score of 100 or more points: 3NT, 4♥, 4♠, 5♣, or 5♦.

game try   The bid of another suit to show a feature of the hand after the trump suit has already been agreed. It's an attempt to reach the game level with a hand of invitational strength.

Gerber Convention   A response of 4♣ to an opening bid of 1NT or 2NT. It asks opener to show the number of aces held.

giving preference   Choosing one of partner's suits.

grand slam   A contract to take all thirteen tricks: 7♣, 7♦, 7♥, 7♠, or 7NT.

high cards   The top four cards in each suit: ace, king, queen, and jack.

high card points (HCPs)   The point-count value given to the high cards in a hand: ace, 4; king, 3; queen, 2; jack, 1.

intermediate jump overcall   A jump overcall showing a good six-card suit and about 14–16 points.

invitational bid   A bid which encourages partner to continue bidding to the game level.

invitational raise   A raise of partner's suit or notrump bid which encourages partner to continue on to the game level or slam level.

jump shift   A bid in a new suit one level higher than necessary. It can be used by opener or responder to show a very strong hand, usually 19 or more points.

jump overcall An overcall in a suit one level higher than necessary. Depending on partnership agreement, it can show a strong, intermediate, or weak hand.

limit bid A bid which describes the strength of the hand within a narrow range of about 3 points. For example, a 1NT opening bid.

limit raise A bidding style in which a jump raise of opener's suit to the three level is invitational, showing about 11–12 points.

major suit Hearts or spades.

minor suit Clubs or diamonds.

negative response An artificial bid used to show a very weak hand. For example, the response of 2NT to an opening strong two-bid.

negative double A type of takeout double, used after the opponents make an overcall during the auction.

opener's rebid Opener's second bid.

overcall A bid made after the other partnership has opened the bidding.

partscore A contract with a trick score of less than 100 points.

penalty double A double made with the intention of increasing the bonus for defeating the contract.

playing tricks The tricks expected to be won from a hand, provided the contract is played in the holder's choice of trump suit.

preemptive opening bid An opening bid in a suit at the three level or higher, showing a long suit and a weak hand.

preemptive raise A jump raise of partner's suit to the four level with good trump support but a weak hand.

quantitative raise An invitational raise.

quick tricks High card holdings in a suit that are expected to win the first or second trick in the suit. For example, the ace and king in a suit represent two quick tricks.

raise Support partner's suit by bidding the suit at a higher level.

redouble A bid that increases the bonuses for making or defeating the contract after it has already been doubled. The redouble may be used as a conventional bid in some situations.

reverse A rebid at the two level or higher in a suit higher-ranking than the one originally bid. It's usually used to show a medium-strength or maximum-strength hand.

sacrificing Bidding to a contract which you don't expect to make to prevent the opponents from playing and making their contract.

short club An opening bid of 1♣ with fewer than four cards in the suit. Frequently used when the hand contains no five-card or longer major suit.

sign-off bid   A bid which partner is expected to pass.

simple overcall   An overcall made at the lowest available level.

singleton   A holding of one card in a suit.

small slam   A contract to take twelve tricks: 6♣, 6♦, 6♥, 6♠, or 6NT.

Stayman Convention   An artificial response of 2♣ to an opening bid of 1NT (or 3♣ to an opening bid of 2NT), asking opener to bid a four-card major suit.

strong two-bid   An opening bid in a suit at the two level that is forcing to the game level.

strong jump overcall   A jump overcall showing a good six-card suit and about 17 or more points.

style   The general partnership agreement on natural bids. For example, the partnership style might be to use five-card majors and weak two-bids, rather than four-card majors and strong two-bids.

support   The number of cards held in a suit bid by partner.

takeout double   A double of an opponent's bid that asks partner to choose another suit as trump.

unbalanced hand   A hand containing a void, a singleton, or more than one doubleton.

unbid suit   A suit that hasn't been bid during the auction.

unusual (two) notrump overcall   A conventional bid to show a two-suited hand in a competitive auction. It usually asks partner to pick a minor suit as trump after the opponents have opened in a major suit.

up the line   The practice of making the cheapest bid when responding or rebidding with a choice of four-card suits.

void   A holding of zero cards in a suit.

waiting bid   A temporizing bid made in anticipation of getting more information about partner's hand.

weak two-bid   An opening bid at the two level in a suit, showing a six-card suit and about 6–10 high card points.

weak jump overcall   A jump overcall showing a long suit and a weak hand.

Scoring

The object of the game is to score points, and this can be done in two ways: *trick score* and *bonus points*. Bridge can be scored using different formats, the three most common being *rubber, duplicate,* and *Chicago*. While the trick score remains the same in all forms of the game, the way the bonuses are awarded can vary. Since rubber bridge scoring is the basis for the other formats, we'll start with that and then discuss the differences in duplicate and Chicago scoring.

Rubber Bridge Scoring

The trick score points are accumulated to produce *games*. The first partnership to win two games wins the *rubber.*

The Score Sheet

The points scored by both sides are recorded on a score sheet which looks like this:

	WE	THEY
Above the line ▶	500	30
Below the line ▶	100	
		120
	80	
	40	
Totals ▶	720	150

As you might expect, points won by your side go under the "We" column, and points scored by the other side go under the "They" column. The horizontal line about half way down the sheet separates the trick score from the bonuses. Trick scores go below the line; bonuses are entered above the line.

Trick Score

If declarer makes the contract, points are awarded for the **contracted** number of tricks as follows:

Clubs (♣) and diamonds (♦) 20 points per trick.

Hearts (♥) and spades (♠)   30 points per trick.

Notrump   40 points for the first trick and 30 points for each subsequent trick.

For example, if you take nine tricks in a contract of 3♥ you get a trick score of 90 points below the line.

Overtricks

If you take ten tricks in your 3♥ contract you still get a trick score of 90 points below the line, but the 30 points for the extra trick—the *overtrick*—are scored as a bonus above the line.

Game

You score a game when you get 100 or more points below the line. This can be done in a single hand, by bidding to a *game contract* worth 100 or more points. 3NT, 4♥, 4♠, 5♣, and 5♦ are the minimum contracts in each denomination that are worth 100 or more points. A contract worth less than 100 points is called a *partscore*. A game can also be scored by accumulating two or more partscores that add up to 100 or more points.

As soon as one side scores a game, a line is drawn on the score sheet below the trick scores. Both sides must start again to accumulate the 100 points needed for a game.

Vulnerability

A side which scores a game is referred to as being *vulnerable*. This has an effect on any subsequent bonus points that are awarded.

Rubber Bonus

The first side to score two games wins the rubber. A bonus of 700 points is awarded if the rubber is won two games to none. A bonus of 500 points is awarded if the rubber is won two games to one.

If you stop playing before a rubber is complete, you get a bonus of 300 points for a game and 100 points for a partscore in an unfinished game.

Slam Bonus

The bonuses awarded for bidding and making a small slam (6♣, 6♦, 6♥, 6♠, or 6NT) or a grand slam (7♣, 7♦, 7♥, 7♠, or 7NT) depend on the vulnerability as follows:

	Nonvulnerable	*Vulnerable*
Small Slam	500	750
Grand Slam	1000	1500

Undertricks

The side that defeats a contract receives a bonus above the line for each trick—*undertrick*—by which the contract was defeated. The bonus depends on the vulnerability as follows:

Nonvulnerable	*Vulnerable*
50 points per undertrick	100 points per undertrick

Doubles and Redoubles

The effect of doubles and redoubles is to increase the scores for making or defeating the contract.

If a doubled contract is made, the trick score below the line is doubled, and a bonus of 50 points is awarded. The bonus for any overtricks depends on the vulnerability as follows:

Nonvulnerable	*Vulnerable*
100 points per overtrick	200 points per overtrick

If a doubled contract is defeated, the defenders' bonus for each undertrick depends on the vulnerability as follows:

Nonvulnerable	*Vulnerable*
100 points for the first undertrick	200 points for the first undertrick
200 points for the second undertrick	300 points for each undertrick thereafter
200 points for the third undertrick	
300 points for each undertrick thereafter	

If a redoubled contract is made, the trick score below the line is multiplied by four, and a bonus of 100 points is awarded. The bonus for any overtricks is twice the doubled bonus.

If a redoubled contract is defeated, the defender's bonus for each undertrick is twice the doubled bonus.

Honors

There are five trump honors, the ace, king, queen, jack, and ten. If one player holds any four of these, the partnership gets a bonus of 100 points. If one player holds all five of the trump honors, the partnership gets a bonus of 150 points. In a notrump contract, a bonus of 150 points is given if one player holds all four aces.

Duplicate Scoring

The primary difference in scoring between duplicate bridge and rubber bridge is that there's no rubber bonus. The vulnerability on each hand in duplicate scoring is predetermined. In place of the rubber bonus, a bonus for making the contract is awarded at the end of each hand based on the vulnerability as follows:

	Nonvulnerable	*Vulnerable*
Partscore contract	50 points	50 points
Game contract	300 points	500 points

The trick score and all other bonuses remain the same, with the exception that there's no bonus for honors in duplicate bridge.

Chicago Scoring

Chicago, or *four-deal bridge,* is an abbreviated form of rubber bridge. Since a rubber of bridge might continue for many hands—until one side scores two games—the Chicago format is used to limit each rubber, or *chukker,* to four deals. At the end of four deals, the players can change partners or move to another table if there are several tables in play.

Chicago is scored in a similar manner to rubber bridge with two exceptions. First, the vulnerability on each of the four deals is determined as follows:

First deal—Both sides nonvulnerable.

Second and third deal—Dealer's side vulnerable, other side nonvulnerable.

Fourth deal—Both sides vulnerable.

If all four players pass, the hand is dealt out again by the same dealer.

The second change is that there's no rubber bonus. Instead, a bonus of 300 points is immediately awarded for making a nonvulnerable game and a bonus of 500 points is awarded for a vulnerable game—similar to duplicate scoring. As in rubber bridge, partscores can be accumulated to score a game. A partnership gets a bonus of 100 points on the fourth deal if it makes a partscore that isn't sufficient to score a game.

This is a good format to use for a party bridge game at home when there are two or more tables of players. There's a break at the end of every fourth hand, which provides lots of opportunity to socialize.

Four-Card Majors

Many partnerships prefer the bidding style of four-card majors to that of five-card majors. In both styles, the longest suit is opened when it contains five or more cards. When there's no five-card or longer suit, those using the five-card major approach will open the bidding in a minor suit. Players using the four-card major approach can open the bidding at the one level in a four-card major suit.

Chapter 4 highlights some differences between the styles, and the remainder of the book adheres to the five-card major approach. This appendix includes a few more details for those favoring the four-card major style.

Partnerships using four-card majors have fewer guidelines to remember when opening the bidding because they generally open their longest suit. Nonetheless, there are some variations within this approach.

♠ 9 8 7 4
♥ K Q 6
♦ A 6 5
♣ A J 4

Even dedicated adherents to four-card majors sometimes prefer not to open poor four-card major suits—those with fewer than 4 HCPs in the suit. This hand might be opened 1♣ in either the four-card or five-card major style.

With a choice of four-card suits, there's no universal agreement on the best suit to open. Rather than the higher-ranking of two four-card suits, some players prefer to open the lower-ranking four-card suit, or the four-card "suit below the doubleton".

♠ K Q 9 6
♥ A Q J 2
♦ J 9 8
♣ 5 2

The modern style is to open this type of hand 1♥, rather than 1♠
Players who open the suit "below" the doubleton have to do some
mental gymnastics on this hand. Since there's no suit below clubs,
they would circle around to the top and open 1♠. Of course, those
playing five-card majors would open the "better" minor, 1♦. Chalk
one up for four-card majors!

With three four-card suits, the middle-ranking is usually opened:

♠ K J 6 3
♥ 4
♦ Q J 7 3
♣ A Q 8 2

This hand would usually be opened 1♦, rather than 1♣. This is the
same opening bid that the five-card major advocates would make.

Bi-Monthly Newsletter

Audrey Grant's Better Bridge Newsletter, which keeps you informed on what's happening in the world of bridge today. There are articles on a wide variety of topics including play, defense, bidding conventions, famous hands, bridge etiquette, and bridge history.

For a year's subscription, send $19.95 (U.S. dollars) and your name and mailing address to:

Better Bridge Newsletter
11333 Moorpark St., Suite 458
Studio City, California 91602

Cruises and Seminars

Audrey Grant's Better Bridge Cruises and Tours™, are offered regularly. Details can be obtained from:

Audrey Grant's Better Bridge Cruises and Tours™
Empress Bridge Cruises and Tours
1-800-724-1386; FAX: 607-785-9919

Bridge Supplies

Randy Baron produces a full-color catalog of bridge supplies, including a selection of cards and other specialties. The American Contract Bridge League also has a catalog offering bridge supplies.

Baron-Barclay Bridge Supplies
3600 Chamberlain Lane, Suite 230
Louisville, KY 40241
1-800-274-2221; 502-426-0410; FAX: 502-426-2044

The American Contract Bridge League
Order Department—The Bridge Source
2990 Airways Blvd.
Memphis, TN 38116-3847
1-800-264-2743; FAX: 901-398-7754